Edition: André Boccato
Graphic Project: Casa do Design - Camilla Frisoni Sola and Luiz Flavio Giannotti
Art Direction: Casa do Design   **Designer:** Ed Edison
Photography Direction: Camilla Frisoni Sola
Editorial Coordination: Rita Pereira de Souza
Cover: Opening image by the artist Dimas Bontempo
Recipes: Morena Leite
Portuguese-English Translation: Fabiana Tsukahara and Lucimeire Vergilio Leite
Photos: Boccato Estúdio Fotográfico - Emiliano Boccato / Paulo Bau - page 48
Photos Sambaphoto: Ed Viggiani - page 18 / Angelo Pastorello - page 19 / André Rolim - page 66 / Iatã Cannabrava - page 111 / Ana Cê - page 131 / Marcelo Reis - pages 138 and 139 / Helô Passos - pages 160 and 161 / Claudia Jaguaribe - pages 49, 67, 110 and 130
Image Edition: Leandro Fonseca and Carlos Pedretti
Production: Karen Sakai and Airton G. Pacheco
Objects: Stella Ferraz Cerêmica and Ritz Festa
Capim Santo Team: Morena Leite

Daniela Venturi, Jandes Morais, Eduardo dos Santos, Neide Motta, Joaquim Portela, Zeca dos Santos, Antonio Dias, Rose Cruz, Sonia Ferreira, Vera Bittencourt, Junior de Oliveira, Aurinete Morais - "Alvinha", Elinton Aparecido, Genivaldo da Silva, Ivonete Bittencurt, Ricardo Neves and Erlon Miranda

Editora Boccato
Administration: Maria Aparecida C. Ramos
Art Direction: Eduardo Schultz
Administrative Assistant: Cenair Streck
Marketing: Marcel Mariano Grego dos Santos
Editora Gaia
Publishing Director: Jefferson L. Alves
Marketing Director: Richard A. Alves
CD recording: produced by Maurício Tagliari / except "Menino das Laranjas", produced by André Magalhães / A & R: Maurício Tagliari / technical direction: Carlos "Cacá" Lima / label manager: Chico Urbanus / recorded by Gustavo Lenza at YB Studio (São Paulo), except "Menino das Laranjas" recorded at Zabumba Studio (São Paulo) / mixed and mastered by Carlos "Cacá" Lima at YB Sudio
Printed by Geográfica Editora

Editora Boccato
Rua dos Italianos, 845 - Bom Retiro
01131-000 - São Paulo - SP - Brasil
(11) 3846-5141
editora@boccato.com.br

Editora Gaia Ltda.
(of the group Global Editora & Distribuidora Ltda.)
Rua Pirapitingüi, 111-A - Liberdade
01508-020 - São Paulo - SP - Brasil
(+55 11) 3277-7999
www.globaleditora.com.br - gaia@editoragaia.com.br
Catalogue number: 2807

Cataloguing in Publication (CIP) International Data
(Brazilian Book Chamber, São Paulo, Brazil)

Leite, Morena
  Brazil, rhythms and recipes / Morena Leite. --
2nd edition -- São Paulo: Gaia: Editora Boccato, 2006.

  Various collaborators.
  Including audio CD/
  ISBN 978-85-7555-11-03

  1. Cuisine 2. Brazilian cuisine 3. Recipes
I. Title.
06-4668   CDD-641.5981

Index to systematic catalogue:
1. Brazil: Cuisine: Domestic economy
    641.5981

© **Copyright Editora Boccato** – All rights reserved. Recipes here presented are entitled to Morena Leite and Editora Boccato, and can not be reproduced (in print or digital format) without the permission of the holders. All recipes have been tested, but its elaboration remains a personal interpretation. Photographic images of recipes are artistic illustrations and do not aim to reproduce exact proportions. Therefore, Editora Boccato and the author can not be held accountable for possible differences in the preparation of recipes.

Brazil, Rhythms and Recipes

Morena Leite

"BEST INNOVATIVE FOOD BOOK IN THE WORLD"
GOURMAND WORLD COOKBOOK AWARDS

Gourmand World Cookbook Awards is a highly prestigious, competitive international award in the gastronomy publications sector. It was created in 1995 by Edouard Cointreau, whose goal is, among others, to spotlight those who can "better cook with words".

Since its creation, the number of participants from different countries has been increasing year after year, along with the quality of its publications: in 2005, about 6.000 books were submitted, representing 65 countries.

Among so many contestants, the winner, considered the best of the world, was the book Brazil, Rythms and Recipes, in its French version, Brésil, Sons et Savours, edited for the celebrations of the Year of Brazil in France – 2005. It was considered the word`s best innovate food book of in the world. With great satisfaction and pride, we, editors and all Brazilians, now share the award with you in this English edition.

BOCCATO PUBLISHING HOUSE
GAIA PUBLISHING HOUSE

brazilian menu

- party pieces — p. 20
- appetizers and salads — p. 52
- entrées — p. 68
- desserts — p. 114
- history — p. 134
- glossary — p. 139
- track list — p. 142

 **To my mother and father...** to whom I owe my life and with whom

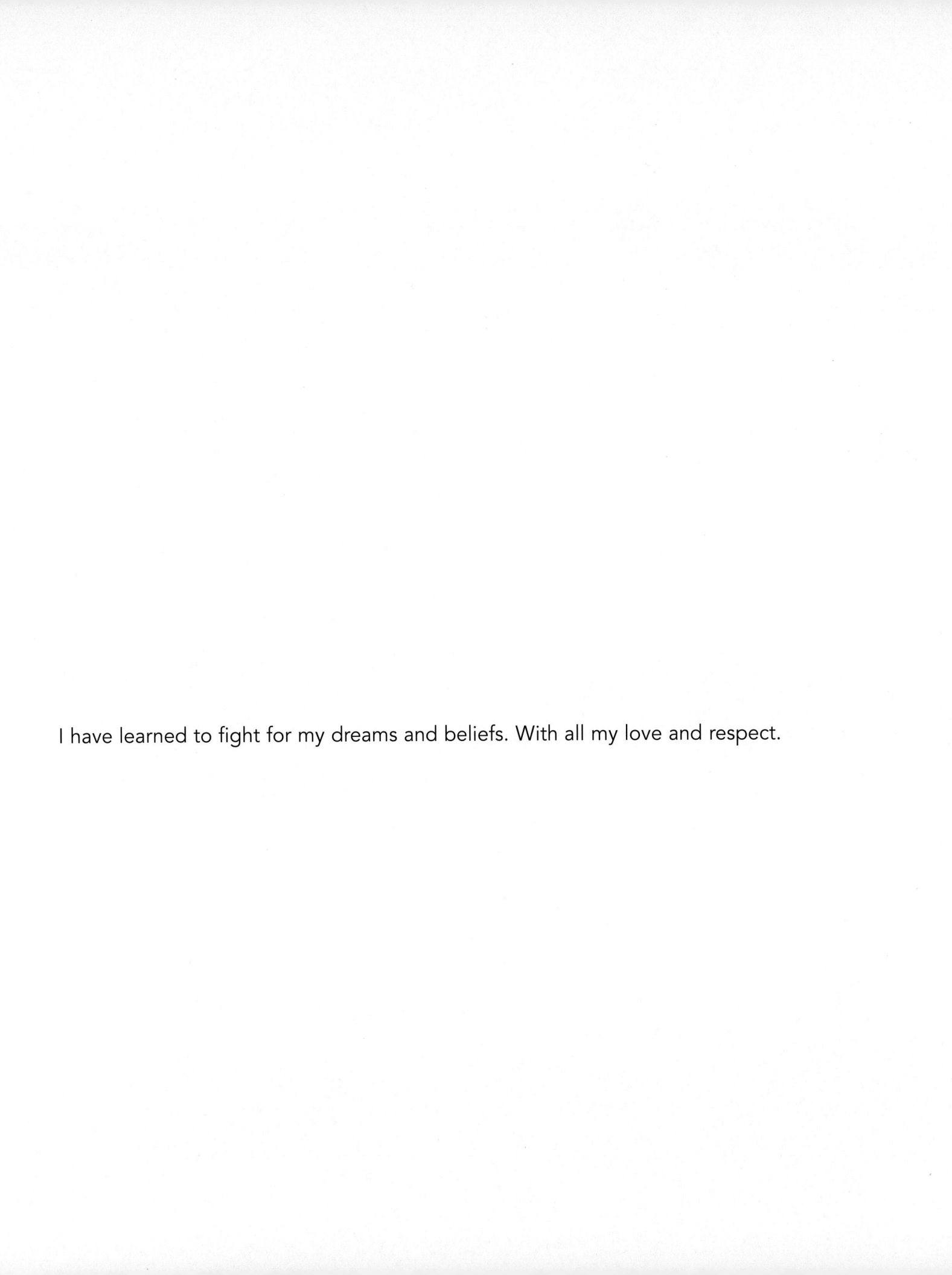

I have learned to fight for my dreams and beliefs. With all my love and respect.

Different people for an unique cuisine

In 1500, the first Portuguese settlers dropped anchors in the north-east of Brazil, later to become the state of Bahia: there was discovered a rich tropical land, inhabited by natives. Since the Portugueses couldn't get the Indians to do the harvest labor, they brought African slaves to work in the sugarcane plantations. It didn't last long until the first mestizos were born. Just like them, our gastronomy is the result of that mix between Europe, Africa and the New World: while the Portuguese brought the use of olive oil, rice, cake and pudding, the African slaves invented the now so traditional feijoada and many other recipes perfumed with the oil of the dende palm, imported from Africa. Then, the Indians bring brought with them the flavours of the New World: how to use exotic fruits like coconut, sweet corn or cashew nut; how to forage herbs, peppers and seeds of the forest; and most of all, how to pound cassava flour in mortals. Cassava has always been used as a sorcerer: various tribes flavored their stew and fish dishes with it. After they discovered it, the Portuguese added it to almost everything: sugarcane syrup, jerked beef, stewed beans… Nowadays, the cassava's flour is the main ingredient of the beiju, a traditional pancake consumed all around the country.

As southern lands were explored, new plantations and tastes were discovered. In the states of Minas Gerais and São Paulo for example, sweet corn has been widely planted and, from sweet stews to porridge, was eaten in its most various forms. As conquerors, leaving the coast behind, plodded through the forest, they

Rediscovering Trancoso, the corner of the wor[ld]

When the Portugueses arrived to the actual Trancoso, it was an Indian land. [The] Africans had to make it their home too. The village was first baptized Aldeia de S[ão João] Batista by the Jesuits, who were later expelled by the Portuguese Crown who fou[nded the] Village of Trancoso.

Built on the plains, overlooking sea cliffs, beaches of thin white sand outlined by [coconut] trees and a dark, calm sea, the village has a rectangular shape. The historical Quadrad[o (mean]ing 'square' in Portuguese) has been built with 25 adobe houses on each side, and [a square] and a church on each end. And so it is today. But since then, different lost biriban[dos have] passed by. In the local slang, biribando is someone coming from another place. Many [of those] who arrived have also lingered, spreading different religions, languages and custom[s, which] has brought such good vibrations to Trancoso and its charismatic people.

Despite this coming and going, the village was rediscovered only at the end of [the 1970's] with the arrival of young idealist intellectuals who had left the cities in search of s[implicity] and quietness. Back then, the village did not have electricity, neither radio or shop[s. Little] by little, its naturalistic cuisine has been modernized, and is now adding to the a[llure of] this truly Brazilian hot spot.

The ambiance of Trancoso is a crossover between the 1950's St. Tropez - when it [was] the hideaway for Parisians intellectuals and rich Americans - and the 1970's hippie [era. It] has beautiful houses, golf courts, old-time hippie communities throwing parties w[ith elec]tronic music, fashionable and international people who still meet at the Quadrado t[o watch] the starts.

At one end of the Quadrado, Capim Santo appeared: an inn and restaurant wher[e Sandra] Marques blends flavors from Trancoso and the rest of the world. Yet, the greatest [change] in its cuisine is Sandra's daughter, chef Morena Leite who, after rambling about [the world] brought back new ideas on how to innovate Brazilian gastronomy. Morena has t[wenty-six] years old, lives in São Paulo and loves *forró*, an amazing northeastern rhythm pla[yed with] an accordion, a tambourine, a metal triangle and an agogô - a rattle-like African pe[rcussion] instrument - and which is danced to tightly in pairs.

Trancoso in a unique place, where natives, hippies and people from all tribes s[tay] together. It is a place just like the forró, that got its name from the incorrect pron[unciation] natives reproduced when they heard foreigners describing the dance: for all.

Mariana Aydar dances the local forró and also sings it. She lives in Paris. Mar[iana and] Morena have been friends since the time they lived by the Quadrado and are now [mixing] their universes - music and gastronomy - in this book.

through the forest, they also started to eat more meat, especially game. When, at the end of the 19th century, the slavery was eventually abolished, the melting pot grew stronger: Middle-eastern immigrants made up for the lack of manpower in farms which, by that time, produced more coffee than sugarcane. These new inhabitants of Brazil brought along deep-rooted culinary traditions and even plants that would begin to blossom in the new land. In the early 20th came the Japanese immigrants, adding sake and the use of raw fish to our already very mixed gastronomy. Most of these people scattered around Brazil. Though a lot of Italians and Germans preferred the colder southern air, many remained in São Paulo, the greatest melting pot of all. That is how restaurants from all origins began to sprout during the 20th century, changing the face of the cities: in our cosmopolitan capitals, one can find Japanese, French or German cuisine, as well as Lebanese, Italian or Angolese.

More recently, a more traditional cooking has been rediscovered. The national engouement for everything coming from abroad eventually came to an end: there is now an enthusiastic use of the local products, like jerked beef, yellow yam or cachaça, our sugarcane rum. Famous chefs, such as Morena Leite, have brought the richness of our land back to where it should never have left. Forgotten ingredients, like okra, guava or tapioca, have once again been rescued from oblivion. Now, five hundred years later, we finally give to the native Brazilian ingredients the honors they deserve.

ALEXANDRA FORBES
Journalist and gastronomy critic. Author of books:
Isabella Suplicy - arte em açúcar and Jantares de mesa e cama.

Love, technique and intuition

Morena always says that who is shut to new flavours is shut to life; that we do not only eat with our mouth, but also with our nose and eyes. Her Brazilian contemporary cuisine highlights colors, textures and temperatures, searching for new ways to maximize the scents and flavors of our country, using techniques from various cultures. Since it was in Paris that she acquired the technique to wake senses through her own way of cooking, Morena was deeply influenced by the French cuisine.

She was born and raised among her mother's saucepans and other children in Trancoso. There, she got to meet different travellers of the village, who gave her the certainty that there was so much more to taste, learn and feel. She went to England to study English. She wanted to be a journalist and, ironically, ended up living with a sophisticated gourmet lady who would prepare banquettes and go to famous chefs' restaurants. She always carried a lime along. It was a sort of pamper for Morena, who loves to squeeze a few lime drops into every food.

Details like these made her realize that the food could be her personal link to the world. She then returned to Trancoso and, at the age of 18, went back to Paris to learn traditional gastronomy at the "Le Cordon Bleu" school, whose strong points are the strict technique, the discipline and the organization required for dishes with exact weight. The school's military-like discipline made Morena realize how talented her mother was for being guided not only by exact measures but also by spoonfuls of intuition, for it is necessary to savor flavors to cook well. Morena matched her intuition with the teachings from French cuisine and pâtisserie, obtaining the Grand Diplôme. Back to Brazil at the age of 19, hand in hand with her mother, she was in charge of the new Capim Santo, which had recently opened in São Paulo. She invented recipes that became widely famous for its perfume and smoothness, surprising everyone with the delicious terrines made of Brazilian ingredients. She has been acclaimed by gourmets and critics, and has become a culinary teacher and a respected cook. Capim Santo has been included in the list of the best restaurants in the country. Now, after eight years, Morena feels it is time she shares the secrets, rhythms and flavors with the many people who pass by Brazil and leave with nothing but sweet nostalgia. This is the good reason why this book has a soundtrack, made of great Brazilian songs and performed by Mariana Aydar.

CHRIS MELLO
Columnist for the O Estado de S. Paulo newspaper and Vogue magazine

"To me, cooking is like sharing my love for my neighbour. I manage my team in the kitchen just like I practice my religion because this space is like a temple! I believe that when cooking, we transfer our energy over to the food and that is why I consider the kitchen to be a sacred place, one of union and fellowship, where culture, knowledge and flavors are safeguarded and handed over.

I find it important to use all our senses when we cook: sight to vary the colors; smel to combine the aromas; taste to join the flavors; and audition to listen to the "sounds that touch and cheer our souls", rhythms that make our heart dances, liberating our creations that come from our sixth sense, our intuition. Food nourishes our bodies as much as music nourishes our souls."

MORENA LEITE

[...]
"O Tio Sam está querendo
conhecer a nossa batucada
Anda dizendo que o molho
da baiana melhorou seu prato
Vai entrar no cuscuz, acarajé e abará"

♪ Moraes Moreira, Brasil pandeiro

Plantain rolls with tenderloin : p.20
Pumpkin and jerked beef dolmades : p.22
Whitebait stuffed with shrimp farofa : p.24
Cassava Rösti with smoked catfish : p.26
Cassava croquettes with shrimp : p.28
Stuffed baked crabs : p.30
Squash coins with jerked beef : p.32
Cheese rolls : p.34
Sautéed shrimp with lemongrass roots : p.36
Triad of brigadeiros served on teaspoon : p.38
Miniature quindins : p.40
Coconut cookies : p.42
Cocada : p.44
Lime caipirinha and Lemongrass caipirinha : p.46
Coconut cocktail and Lemongrass refreshment : p.47

PARTY PIECES

Plantain rolls
with tenderloin

1 liter olive oil or soy oil
18 ripe plantains
30 g butter
600 g tenderloin, cut into small cubes
15 g garlic, smashed
200 g onions, chopped
200 ml dark beer
salt and pepper to taste
parsley to taste

♪ Preparation: thinly slice plantains lengthwise and deep fry them. Set aside. Fry garlic until golden brown, add onions and sauté tenderloin until tender. Sprinkle beer and cook until liquid is reduced. Season with salt and pepper; add parsley.

♪ To assemble: put one coffee spoon of chopped meat on every plantain slice and roll it. Heat rolls in the oven before serving.

♪ Servings: 100 portions

♪ Preparation time: 2 hours

Pumpkin and jerked
beef dolmades

30 kale leaves
1 kg jerked beef
500 g kabocha squash
3 garlic cloves, smashed
100 ml clarified butter
200 g onions, sliced
salt and pepper to taste
parsley to taste

♪ Preparation: place jerked beef in a bowl with water to desalt it, changing the water every hour during 4 hours. Boil whole kale leaves in water with a pinch of salt. Set aside. Peel squash and cut it into medium-sized cubes. Sauté them on a skillet with chopped onions and half the butter, until soft. Set aside. Once meat is desalted, cook it for 30 minutes in pressure cooker. Let it cool for a while then shred it roughly with your hands, removing fat. Sauté sliced onions with the remaining butter. Add shredded jerked beef and sprinkle with parsley. Add pumpkin cubes, season with salt and pepper, mix well.

♪ To assemble: cut every kale leaf in four, place a spoonful of squash and meat mixture in the middle and roll dolmades.

♪ Servings: 100 portions

♪ Preparation time: 6 hours

Whitebait stuffed
with shrimp FAROFA

4 kg whitebait
juice of 1 lemon
salt and pepper to taste
6 eggs, lightly beaten
500 g all-purpose flour
2 l oil, for frying

♪ Shrimp *farofa*: 1 kg prawns, peeled / 300 g cassava flour / 100 *ml* olive oil / 2 garlic cloves, smashed / 100 g onions, thinly chopped / 50 *ml* tomato sauce / chopped parsley to taste / salt and pepper to taste

♪ Preparation: clean whitebaits, removing central bones through the back and head. Season with lemon, salt and black pepper; set aside. To prepare the *farofa*, sauté garlic and onion with olive oil, add shrimps and cook for a few minutes. Add tomato sauce, chopped parsley and, finally, the cassava flour, little by little. Season *farofa* with salt and pepper.

♪ To assemble: stuff fish with *farofa* mixture, dip them first in the flour, then in the eggs and then flour again. Deep fry them. Serve hot.

♪ Servings: 100 portions

♪ Preparation time: 3 hours

Cassava Rösti
with smoked catfish

3 kg precooked cassava
1 kg soft-ripened cheese, grated
400 g unsalted butter
salt and pepper to taste
500 g smoked catfish
1 l milk
50 g butter
20 g garlic
200 g onions
100 g red bell peppers
100 g yellow bell peppers
50 g green bell peppers

♪ **Preparation:** to make the *rösti*, grate cassava and cheese on the large holes of a box grater. Mix with butter. Season with salt and pepper. In a baking pan, spread a thin layer of this mixture. Cut it into 2-cm-diameter circles. Bake *rösti* at medium temperature for 15 minutes. Dice catsfish into small cubes and place it in milk for about 4 hours in the refrigerator to desalt. Drain the milk and set the catfish aside. Sauté garlic in butter until golden brown, add onion and bell peppers. Add catfish, season with pepper and add some salt if necessary. Sprinkle with parsley.

♪ **To assemble:** when serving, warm *rösti* and top them with chopped catfish.

♪ **Servings:** 100 portions

♪ **Preparation time:** 6 hours

Cassava croquettes
with shrimp

♪ Dough:
1 kg cassava
1 egg
50 g unsalted butter
salt and pepper to taste
1 pinch grated nutmeg

♪ Preparation: cook cassava and grate it in a food processor. Mix egg and butter. Season with salt, pepper and nutmeg. Mix to obtain an homogeneous dough.

♪ Filling: 100 *ml* olive oil / 50 g garlic, smashed / 100 g onion, thinly chopped / 700 g prawns, peeled / 200 g tomatoes, peeled / 100 *ml* tomato sauce / salt, pepper and parsley to taste

♪ Preparation: fry garlic in olive oil until golden brown, add chopped onion and sauté for a few minutes. Add shrimp and sauté a little more. Add peeled tomatoes and tomato sauce. Season with salt and pepper.

♪ To assemble: place a teaspoon of the dough in the palm of your hand and form it into a shallow cup. Fill it with the shrimp mixture and enclose, forming a ball. Deep fry balls in hot oil and serve immediately.

♪ Servings: 100 portions

♪ Preparation time: 3 hours

Stuffed baked crabs

3 kg crab meat
juice of 3 lemons
100 g unsalted butter
4 garlic cloves, smashed
100 ml dende oil (palm oil)
600 g onions, thinly chopped
3 tomatoes, diced
300 ml coconut milk
160 g parmesan cheese, grated
salt and pepper to taste
parsley to taste

♪ Preparation: sprinkle lemon on crab meat. Fry garlic until brown in dende oil, add onion and crabmeat and sauté for a few minutes. Season with salt and pepper. If prefered, use a hotter pepper. Add tomato and coconut milk, sauté until liquid evaporates and crab meat is embedded with sauce taste. Add parsley. Fill big-size shells with this mixture, sprinkle parmesan cheese.

♪ To assemble: bake it for some minutes until top is crispy and golden. Serve immediately.

♪ Servings: 100 portions

♪ Preparation time: 1 hour and 30 minutes

Squash coins
with jerked beef

2 kg butternut squash
160 ml olive oil, to season
600 g jerked beef
50 g clarified butter
100 g onions, chopped
3 garlic cloves, smashed
salt and pepper to taste
parsley to taste

♪ Preparation: slice squash into 1.5-cm-thick slices then, with a small cutter, cut circles of 2 cm. Scoop out the flesh in the center of the disks. Place disks on a baking pan, season with salt, pepper and sprinkle olive oil on top, and bake for about 10 minutes. Set aside. Place beef in a bowl with water to desalt it for 4 hours, changing water every hour. Once meat is desalted, cook it for 30 minutes in pressure cooker. With a fork, check if meat is tender. Let it cool a little and roughly shred beef with your hands. In a saucepan, sauté garlic and onion with butter. Add shredded jerked beef and sprinkle with parsley.

♪ To assemble: stuff pumpkin with jerked beef. Place it in the oven and heat it for 5 minutes. Serve warm.

♪ Servings: 100 portions

♪ Preparation time: 6 hours

Cheese rolls

1 1/2 kg sweet manioc starch
200 g acid manioc starch
30 g salt
300 ml oil
800 ml warm milk
1k 750 g soft-ripened cheese
6 eggs

♪   Preparation: mix sweet and acid manioc starches and salt in a bowl. In a saucepan, warm the oil and milk; pour this mixture onto dry ingredients, stirring slowly with a wooden spoon. Add eggs one by one and knead dough until smooth. Finally, add grated cheese and mix well. Make small balls with the dough, using a teaspoon, and place them on a greased baking sheet. Preheated oven to 180° C. Bake rolls for about 15 minutes in a greased baking pan.

♪   Servings: 100 rolls

♪   Preparation time: 1 hour

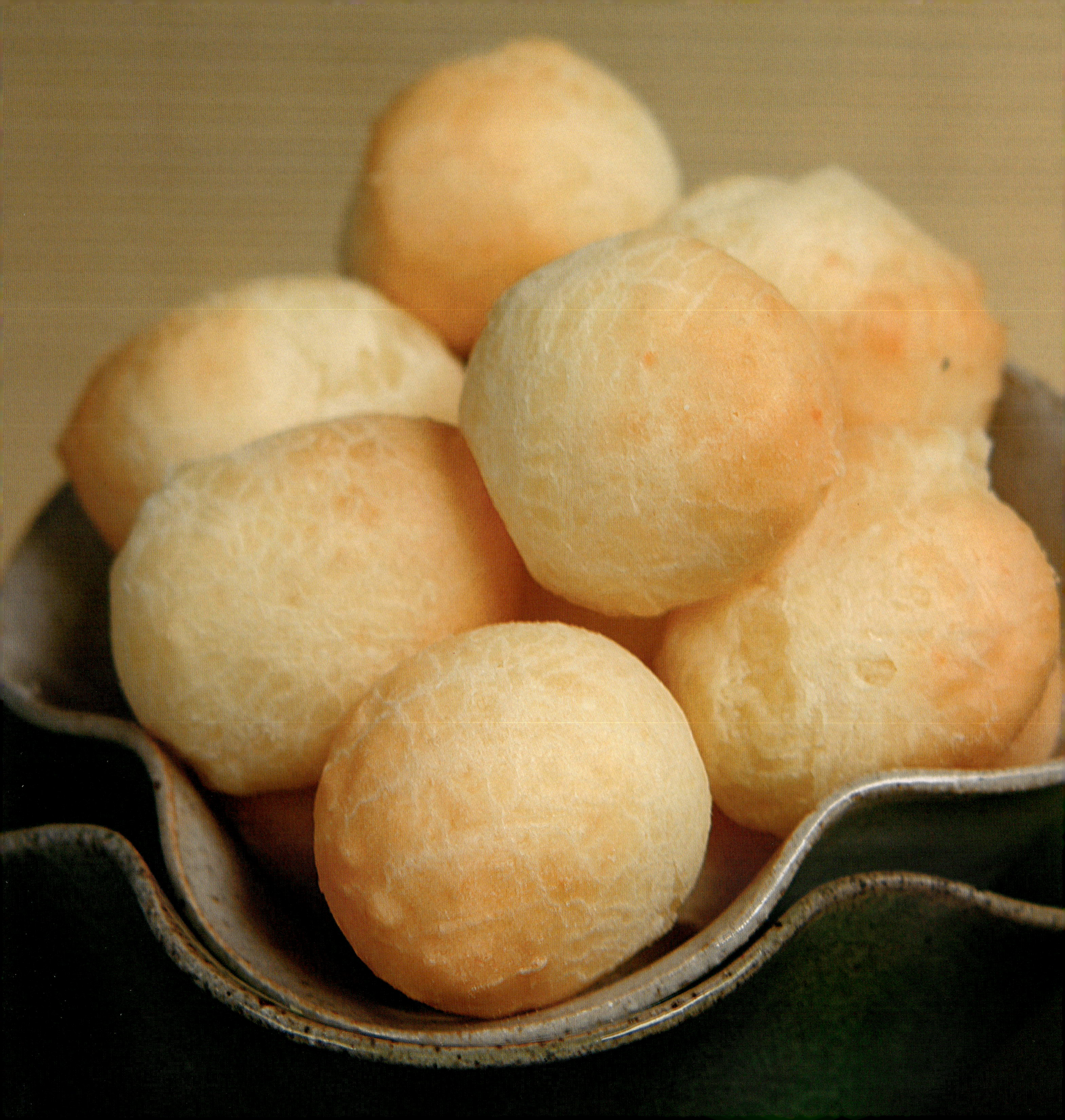

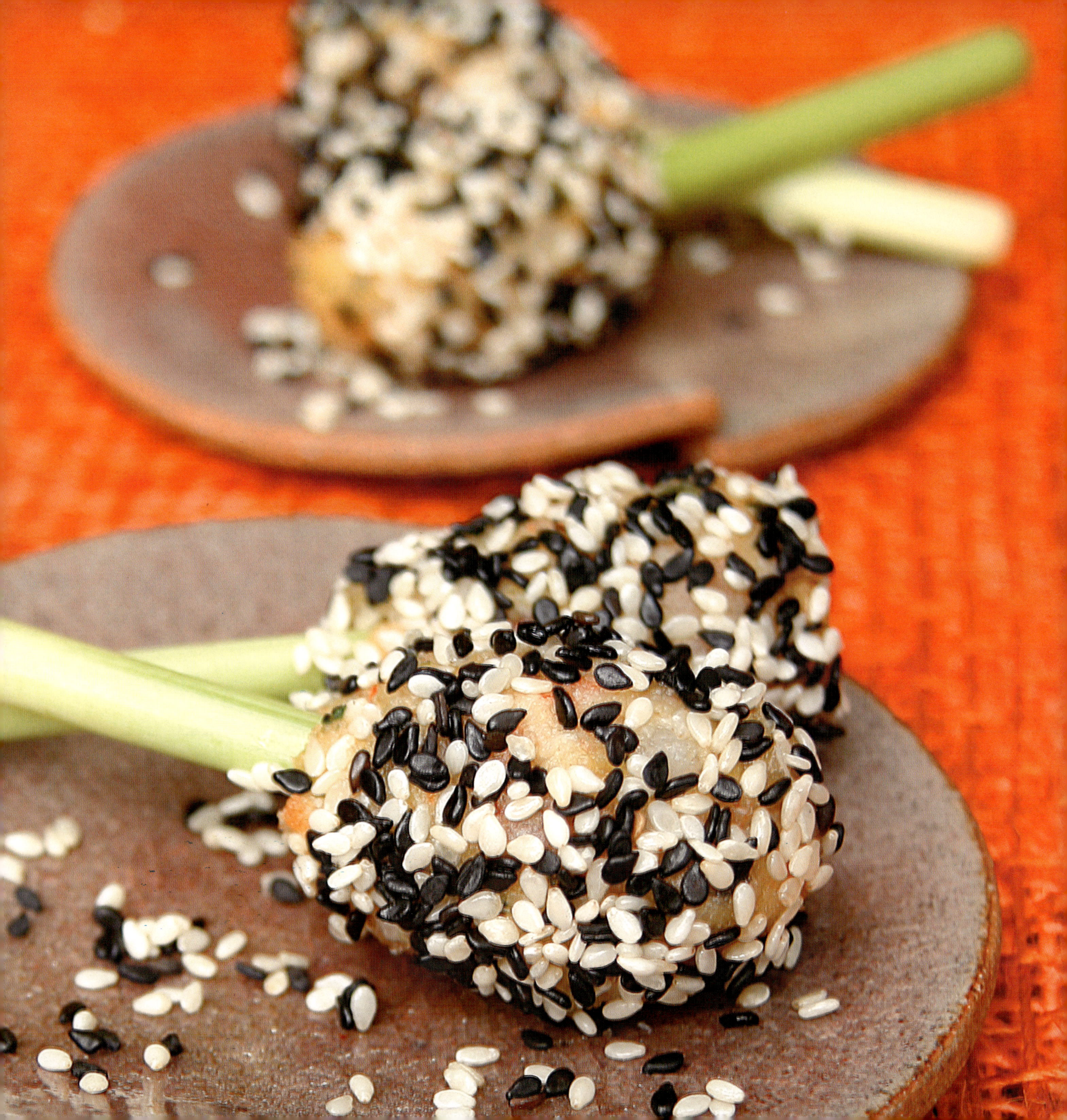

Sautéed Shrimp
with lemongrass roots

2 kg small shrimp, peeled
30 g ginger
2 lemons
1 lime
20 g garlic, smashed
100 g unsalted butter
500 g onions, finely chopped
100 g all-purpose flour
3 egg whites
parsley, basil and mint to taste
100 roots of lemongrass (8 cm)
500 g black sesame seeds
500 g white sesame seeds
salt and pepper to taste

♪ Preparation: season shrimp with salt, pepper, ginger, lemon juice, lemon and lime zests and set aside. In a skillet, sauté garlic in butter. Add onion, salt, pepper and sauté some more. Add this mixture to seasoned shrimp and mix it in a food processor. Transfer shrimp mixture to a bowl and add flour and egg whites. Sprinkle parsley, basil and mint, thinly chopped. Refrigerate for 3 hours, until dough is firm. Roll small balls and stick them with lemongrass roots. Finally, dip balls in mixed sesame seeds and bake them in preheated oven for 15 minutes. Suggestion: Serve with capeta lime sauce.

♪ Capeta lime sauce: 150 g small onion, thinly chopped / 30 g butter / 30 g all-purpose flour / 1 l heavy cream / juice of 4 capeta limes / salt and pepper to taste

♪ Preparation: sauté onion in butter until golden brown, add flour, mix swiftly, adding heavy cream to dissolve it. Boil until it thickens. Add lime juice and season with salt and pepper. Serve with skewers.

♪ Servings: 100 skewers

♪ Preparation time: 4 hours

Triad of *Brigadeiros* served on teaspoon
(chocolate, Brazil nuts and pistachios)

(Brigadeiros *are soft candy balls made with condensed milk; they are very popular in birthday parties in Brazil*)

♪ **Chocolate:**
500 g condensed milk
2 tablespoons unsalted butter
6 tablespoons cocoa powder

♪ **Pistachio:**
500 g condensed milk
2 tablespoons unsalted butter
200 g pistachios

♪ **Brazil nuts:**
500 g condensed milk
2 tablespoons unsalted butter
200 g Brazil nuts

♪ **Preparation:** mix all ingredients and cook at medium heat, stirring constantly until thick.

♪ **Preparation:** place pistachios in a food processor and pulse until they resemble coarse meal. Mix all ingredients and cook over medium heat, stirring constantly until thick.

♪ **Preparation:** place nuts in a food processor and pulse until they resemble coarse meal. Mix all ingredients and cook over medium heat, stirring constantly until thick.

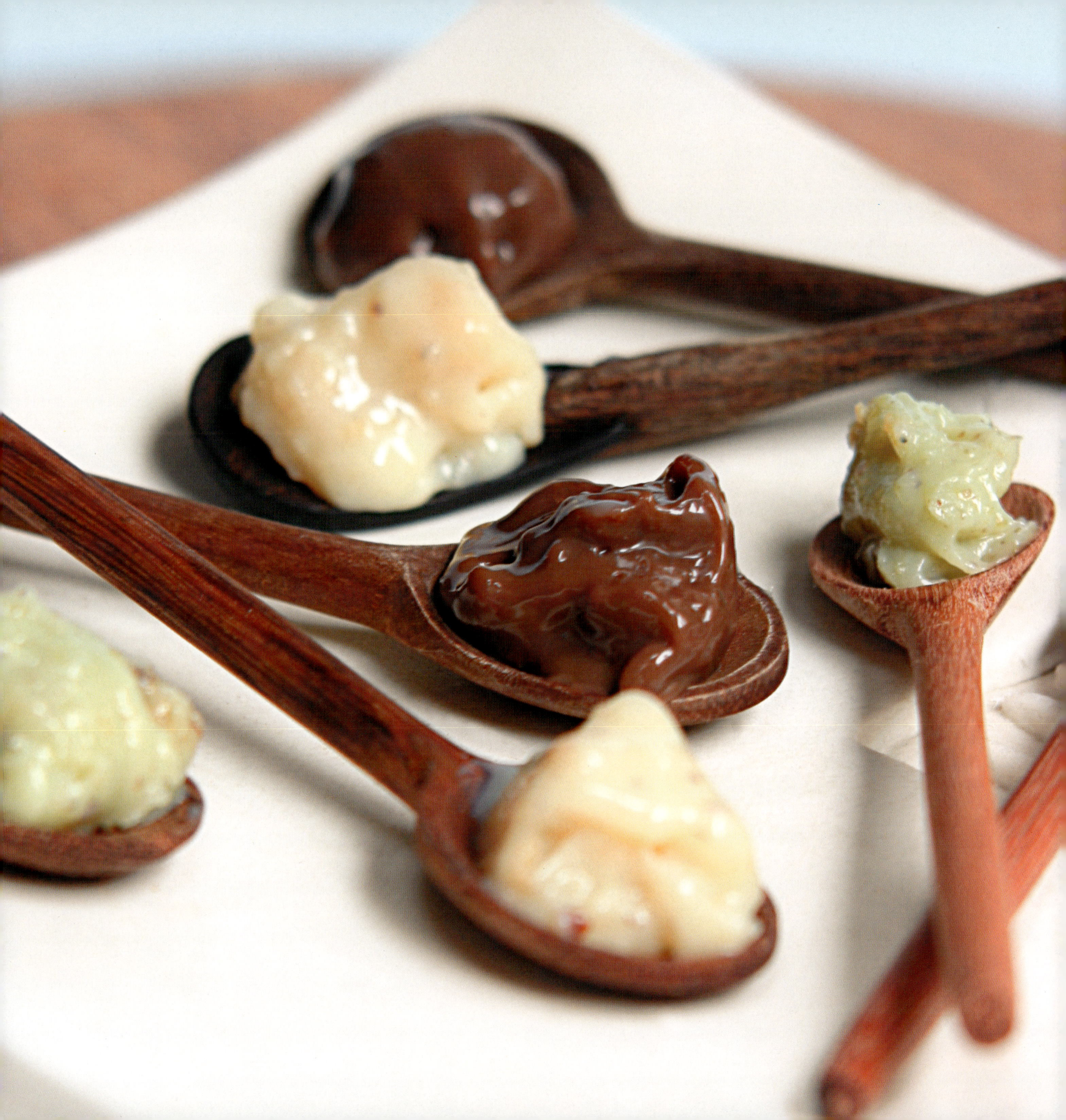

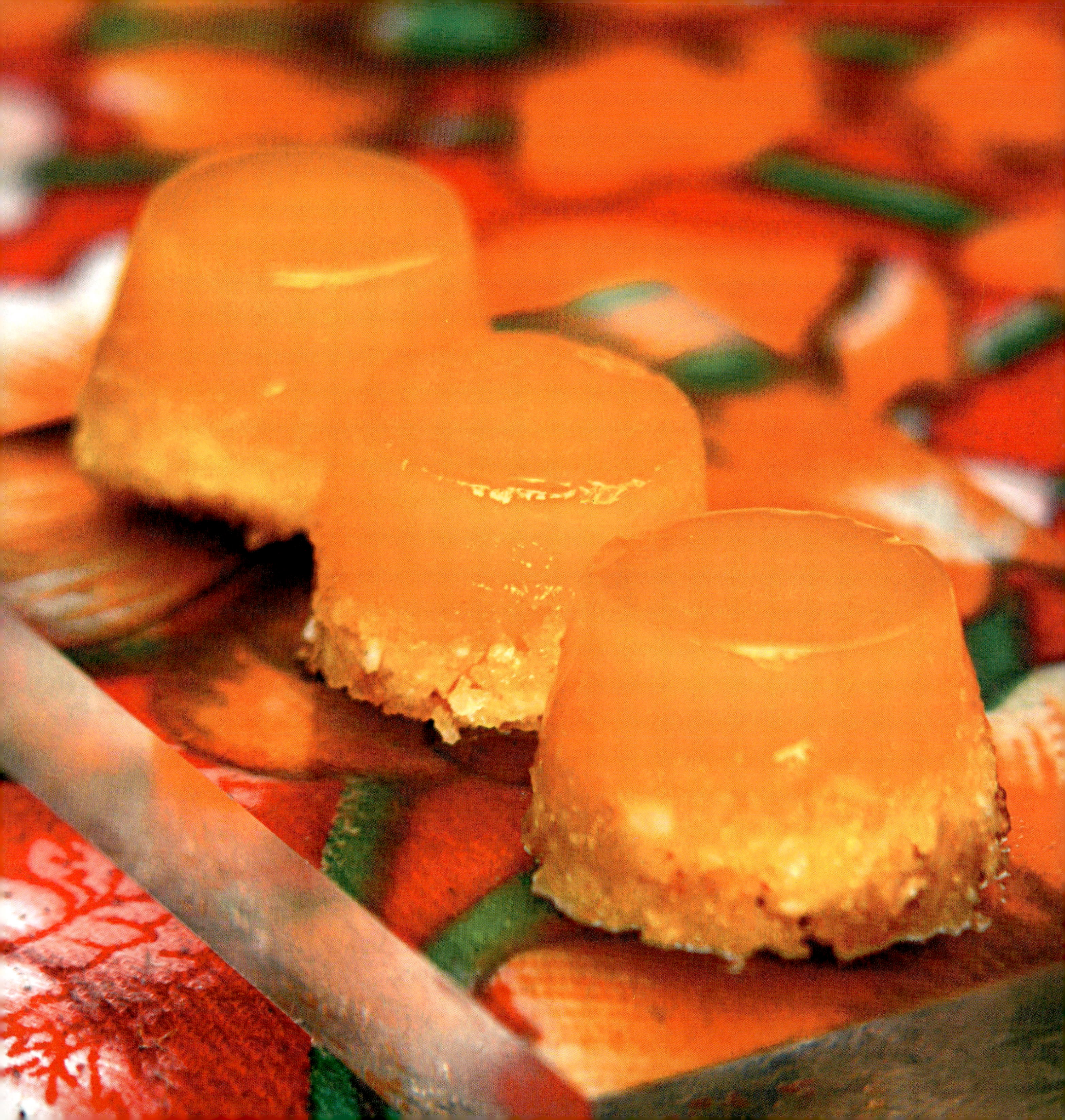

Miniature quindins

Quindins are typical Brazilian tartlets made of yolks and grated coconut

50 g unsalted butter plus
100 g more to grease shells
35 egg yolks
450 g sugar
450 g coconut, grated

♪ Preparation: Mix all ingredients. Grease small tartlet shells with butter and sprinkle sugar. Pour mixture in shells and place them in preheated oven in bain marie~ for 10 minutes. Remove quindins from shells. Serve cold.

♪ Servings: 100 quindins

♪ Preparation time: 1 hour

Coconut cookies

4 cans condensed milk
12 eggs
1 tablespoon unsalted butter
400 g coconut, grated

♪   Preparation: Mix all ingredients and pour mixture into small molds, greased with butter. Bake in preheated oven for about 10 minutes. Remove cookies from molds and serve either warm or cold.

♪   Servings: 100 cookies

♪   Preparation time: 1 hour

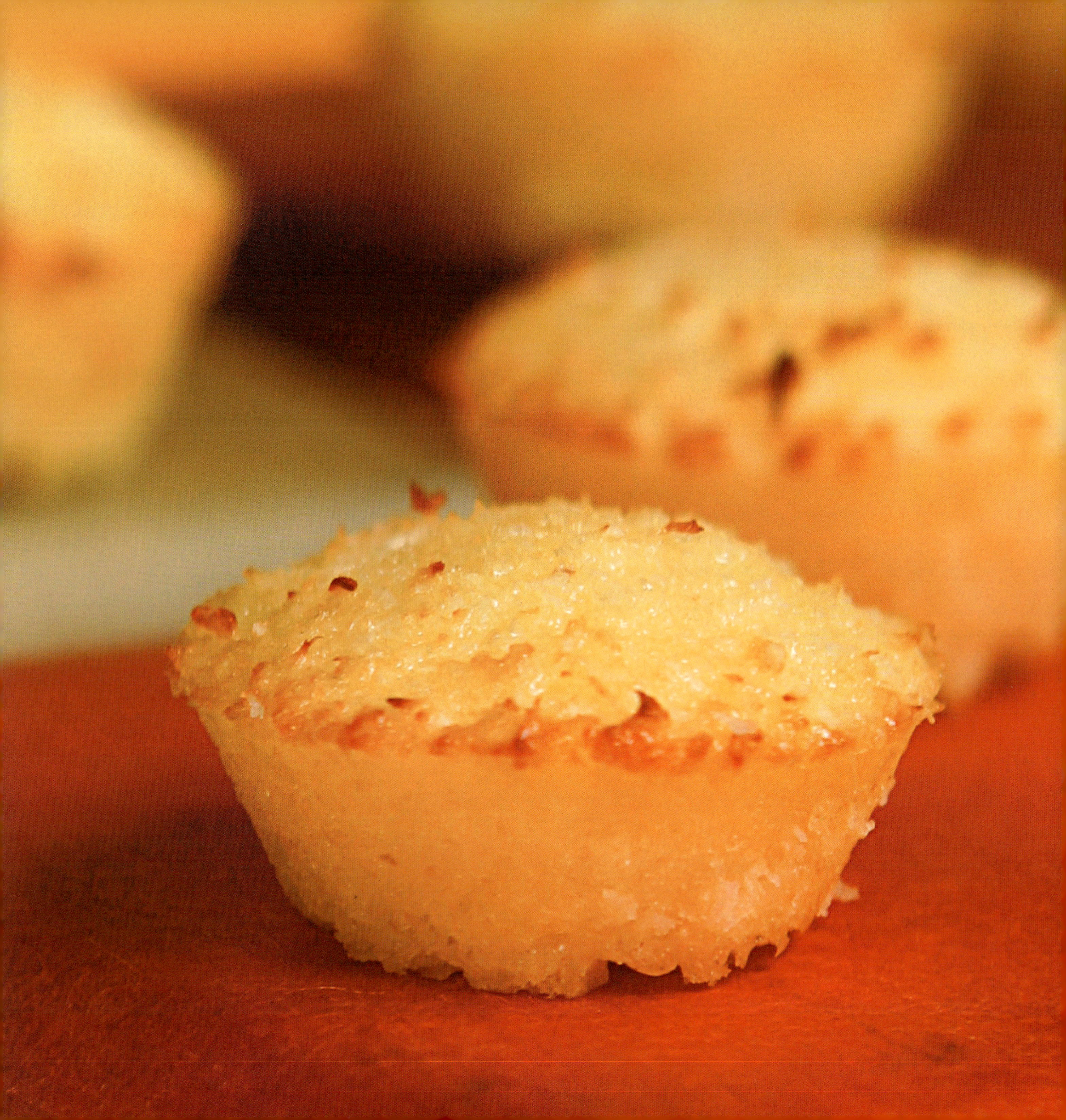

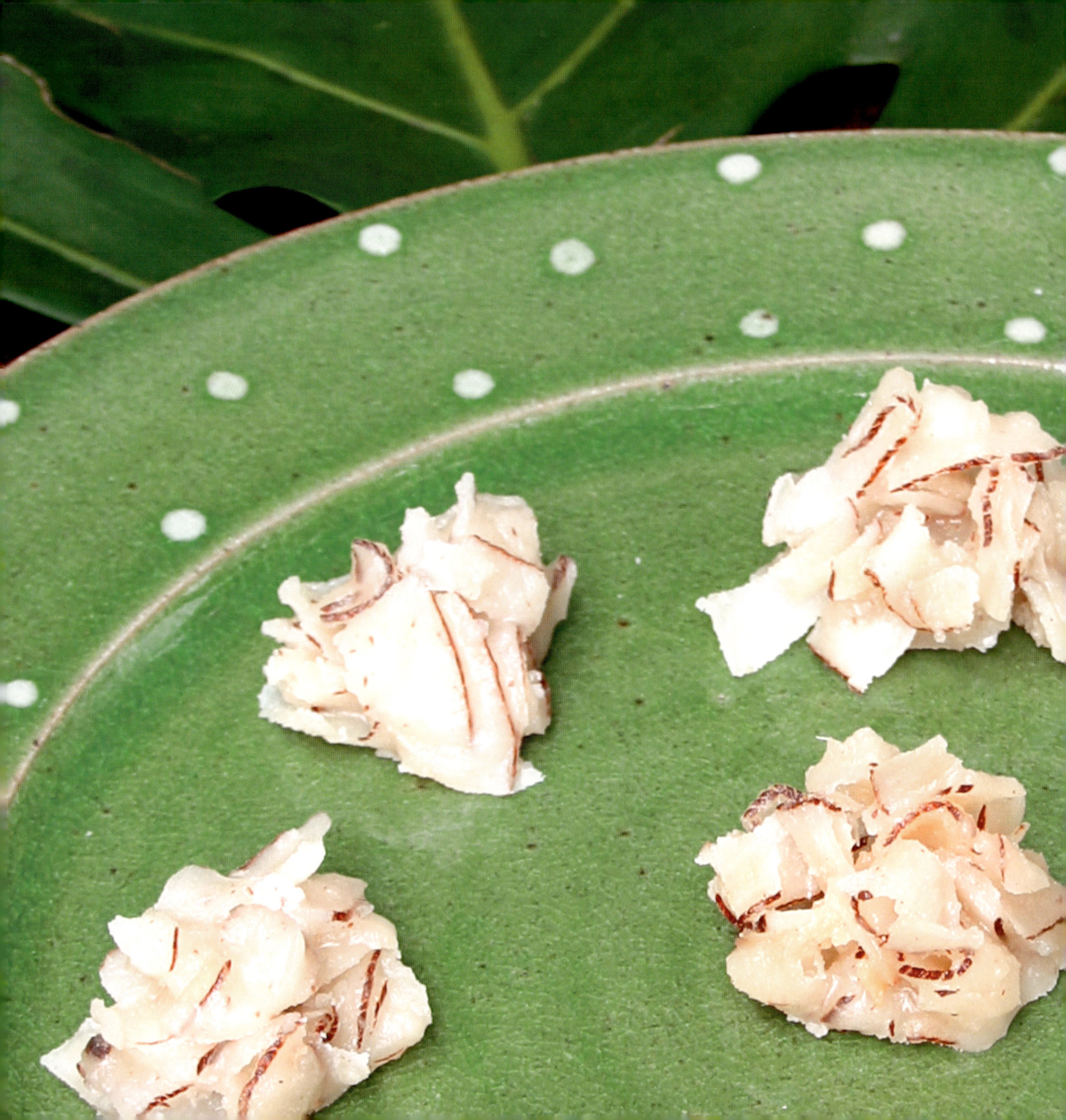

Cocada
(Coconut candy)

1 kg sugar
2 l water
10 cloves
2 kg fresh coconut, grated
150 g unsalted butter
10 egg yolks

♪ Preparation: dissolve sugar in water and add cloves. Bring to a boil until syrup is formed. Do not stir. Add coconut and stir well. Cook over medium heat, constantly stirring, for 5 minutes. Add butter and yolks, mix well and cook until thick. Remove from heat and stir a little more.

♪ To assemble: Using a tablespoon, scoop out bits of coconut sweet and place them on a marble surface. Leave it to cool. Once it gets firm, remove them from marble using a spatula.

♪ Servings: 100

♪ Preparation time: 2 hours

Lime CAIPIRINHA

(Caipirinha is the national drink of Brazil. Its main ingredient is the cachaça, which is a potent sugarcane rum)

10 limes, halved / 350 g sugar / 1 l cachaça or light rum / 1 kg coarsely crushed ice

♪ Preparation: Cut limes in four, add sugar and crush the flesh of the limes using a wooden reamer. Add *cachaça* and ice. Place mixture in a cocktail shaker, close and shake hard.

♪ Servings: 20 tumblers

♪ Preparation time: 15 minutes

Lemongrass CAIPIRINHA

200 g sugar / 200 g lemongrass leaves / juice of 4 limes / 1 l cachaça or light rum / 1 kg coarsely crushed ice / 300 ml water / 400 g lemongrass roots, cut into 20 small sticks for garnish and mix **caipirinha**.

♪ Preparation: Blend water, sugar, lemongrass leaves and lime juice. Strain and transfer to a cocktail shaker and add crushed ice. Close and shake hard.

♪ Servings: 20 tumblers

♪ Preparation time: 15 minutes

Coconut cocktail

1 l cachaça or light rum
2 cans condensed milk
2 l coconut milk
coconut, grated

♪ Preparation: Mix all ingredients in a blender or cocktail shaker. Refrigerate it overnight. When serving, blend again and add some icecubes and sprinkle grated coconut. Serve in a zombie glass with a straw, if prefered.

♪ Servings: 20 glasses

♪ Preparation time: 15 minutes (mixture prepared in advance)

Lemongrass refreshment

200 g lemongrass leaves
2 l water
a few gratings of ginger, to taste
brown sugar, to taste

♪ Preparation: Blend leaves, water and ginger. Strain liquid. Refrigerate. Add brown sugar. Serve very cold.

♪ Servings: 10 glasses

♪ Preparation time: 30 minutes

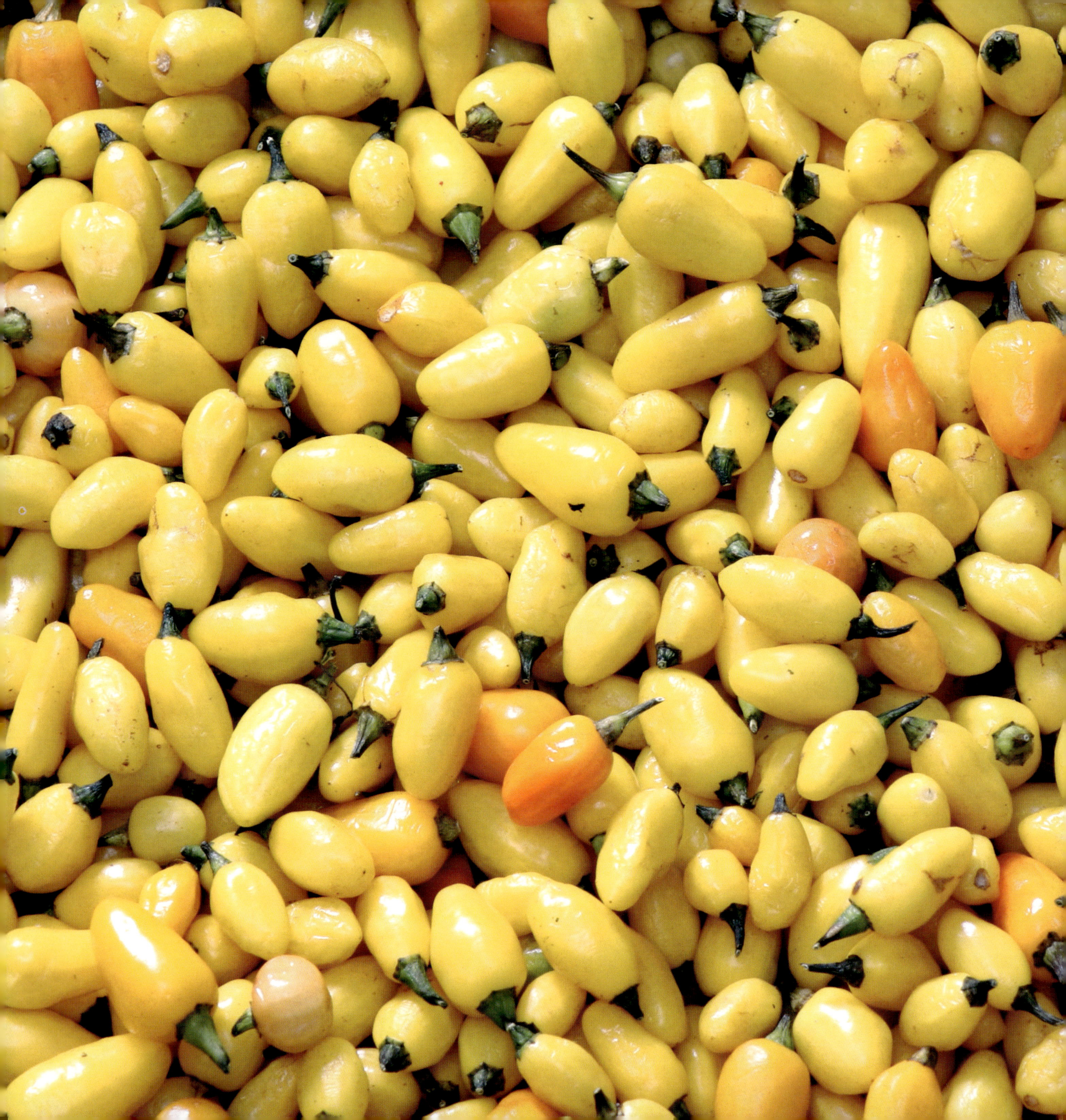

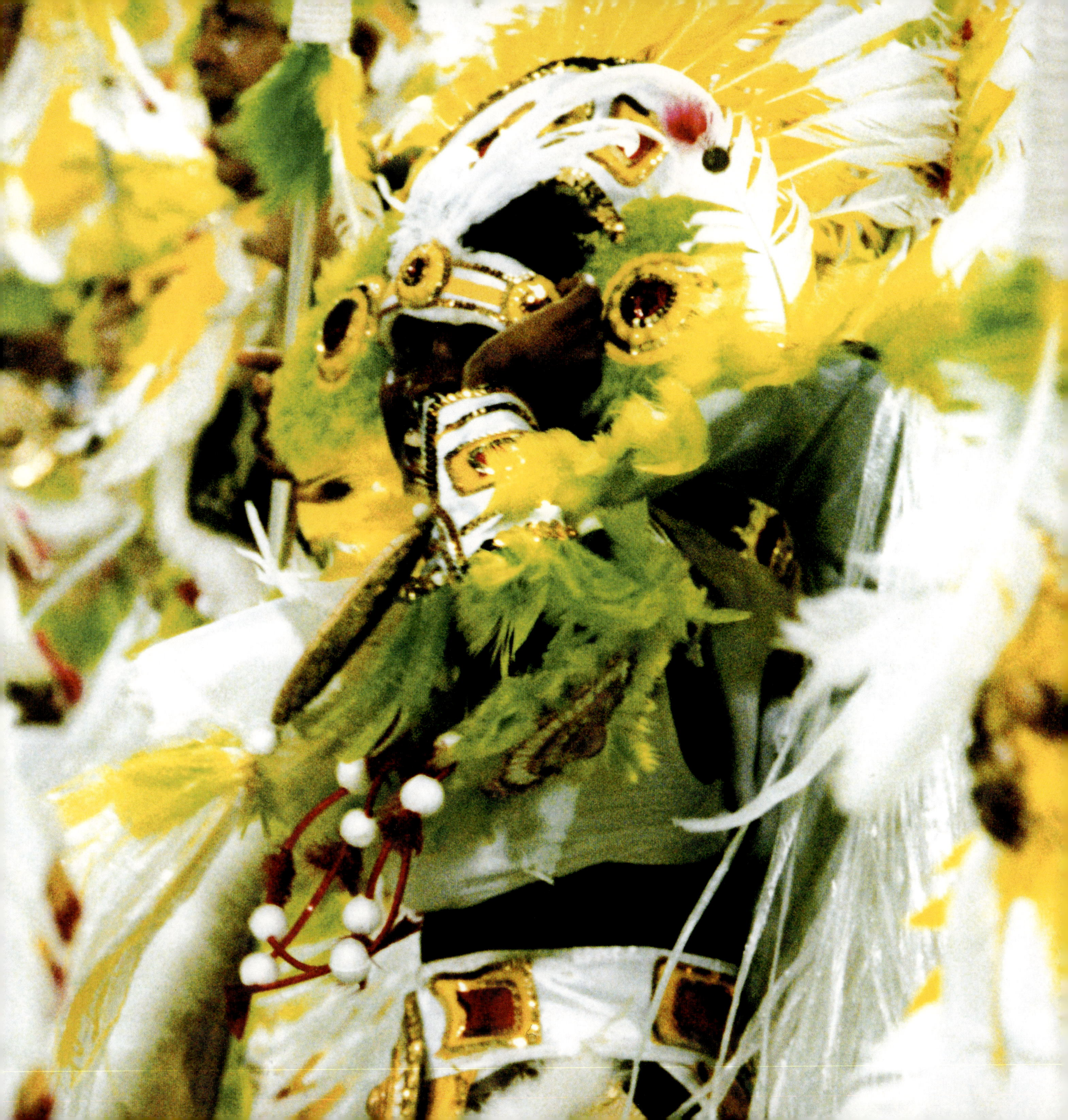

[...]
"Vamos comer

Vamos comer, João

Vamos comer

Vamos comer, Maria

Se tiver

Se não tiver então ô ô ô ô

Vamos comer

Vamos comer canção

Vamos comer

Vamos comer poesia

Se tiver

Se não tiver então ô ô ô ô

♪ Caetano Veloso, "Vamo" comer

Sweet-potato soup with lemongrass : p.52
Crab packages : p.54
Shrimps with tapioca and Brazil nuts : p.56
Snook salad with papaya and peanuts : p.58
Tepid calamari salad : p.60
Beans, tomato and red onion salad : p.62

Appetizers and Salads

Sweet-potato soup
with lemongrass

500 g sweet-potatoes, diced
20 g garlic, smashed
60 g unsalted butter
1 small onion, chopped
60 g lemongrass roots
2 l vegetable broth
salt and pepper to taste
500 ml cream (optional)
parsley to taste

♪ Preparation: sauté garlic in butter until golden brown, then add onion and lemongrass root. Add sweet-potato and pour vegetable broth. Cook until sweet-potato is soft. Blend mixture and place it on a saucepan over heat again. Simmer until it reaches your favorite thickness; season with parsley, salt and pepper. If preferred, add some heavy cream.

♪ To assemble: serve in a tureen or, for a cocktail party, in 20 porcelain spoons.

♪ Servings: 4 portions

♪ Preparation time: 45 minutes

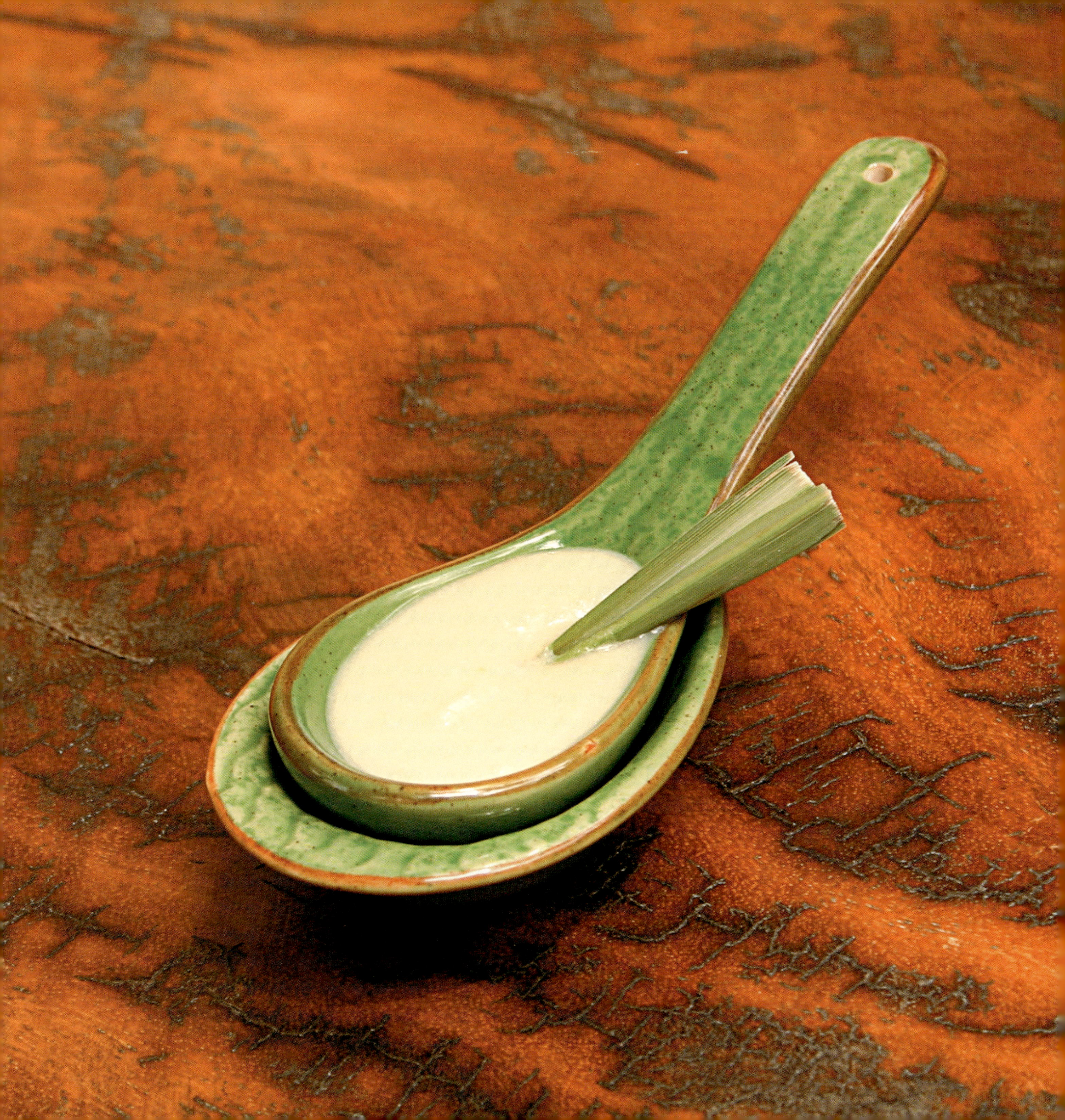

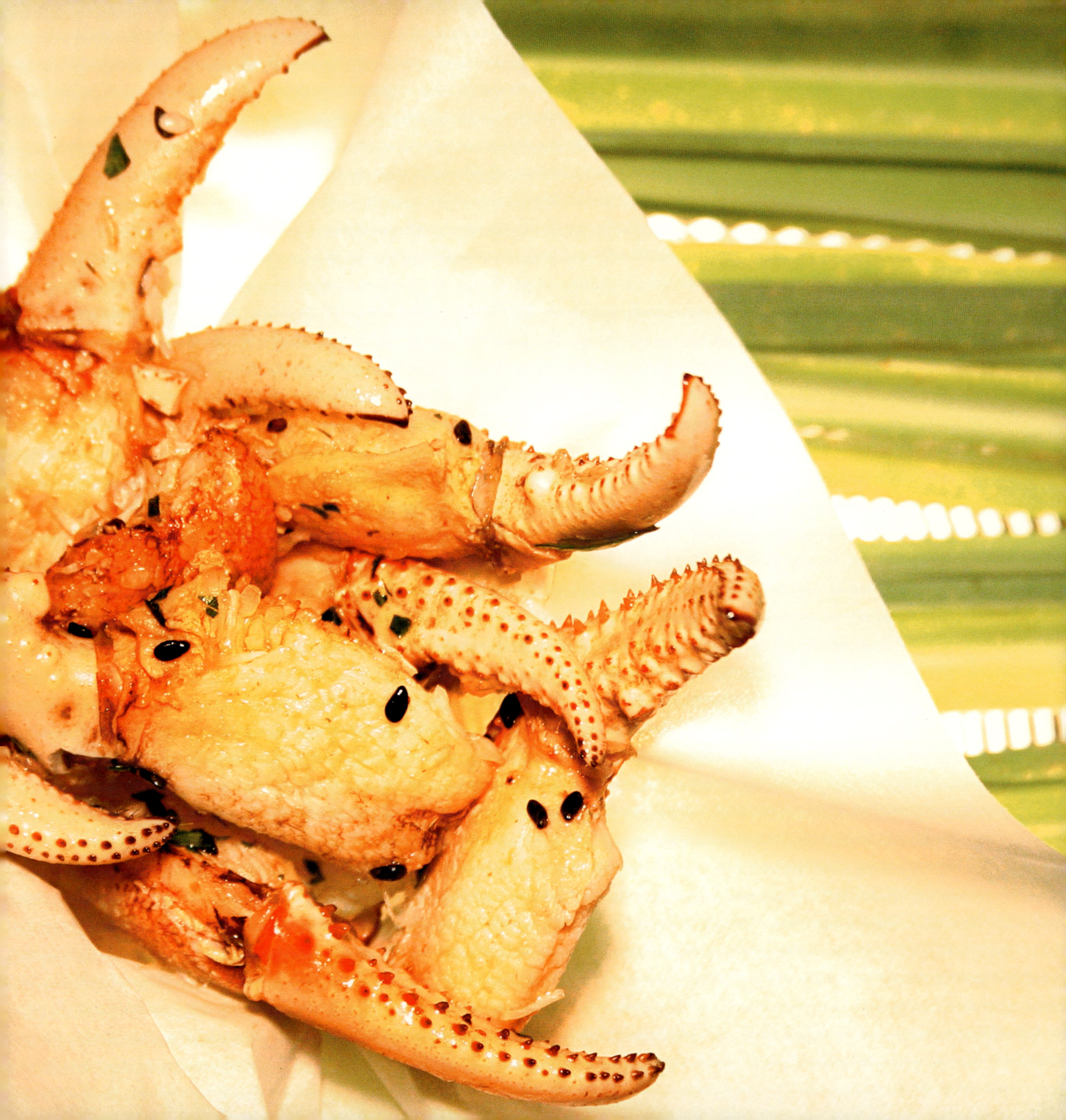

CRAB PACKAGES

♪ **Lemongrass pesto**
30 g cashew nuts, processed into a coarse meal
200 ml olive oil
juice of 2 limes
60 g lemongrass leaves
salt and pepper to taste

♪ **Preparation:** mix all ingredients and blend. Season with salt and pepper to taste.

♪ **Crab mixture:** 640 g crab claws / parchment paper, to wrap / parsley, to garnish / black sesame seeds, to garnish / white sesame seeds, to garnish.

♪ **Preparation:** season crab claws with the pesto and marinate it in refrigerator for 30 minutes. Cut parchment paper in squares of 30 cm x 30 cm. Place claws in the center and sprinkle with pesto. Fold paper like an enveloppe and tightly close all ends so the sauce will not drip out. Place package on a baking sheet, in a preheated oven at high temperature for 10 minutes.

♪ **To assemble:** before serving, open parchment, sprinkle with white and black sesame seeds and parsley. Close package and serve very hot.

♪ **Servings:** 4 portions

♪ **Preparation time:** 50 minutes

Shrimps with tapioca and Brazil nuts

30 g tapioca
100 ml coconut milk
400 ml milk
120 g small shrimps, cleaned
20 g garlic, smashed
1/2 lime
80 g onions
30 g unsalted butter
200 g fresh heart of palms
60 g Brazil nuts
20 g coconut, grated
salt, pepper and lemon juice to taste
parsley and cilantro, chopped, to taste

♪ Preparation: place tapioca in a bowl with 50 ml coconut milk and 200 ml milk, until doubled in size. Season shrimps with salt, pepper and lemon juice. Set aside. Sauté garlic and onion in butter; add shrimps and sauté for some minutes more. Dice hearts of palms and cook until tender. Drain and blend hearts of palms with remaining milk and coconut milk, until a cream is formed; add Brazil nuts previously blended into coarse meal. Place mixture in a saucepan, bring to a simmer and slowly add tapioca, constantly stirring until it thickens. Season with salt and pepper.

♪ To assemble: to serve, pour cream into 4 ramekins, sprinkle grated coconut, chopped parsley and cilantro.

♪ Servings: 4 portions

♪ Preparation time: 1 hour

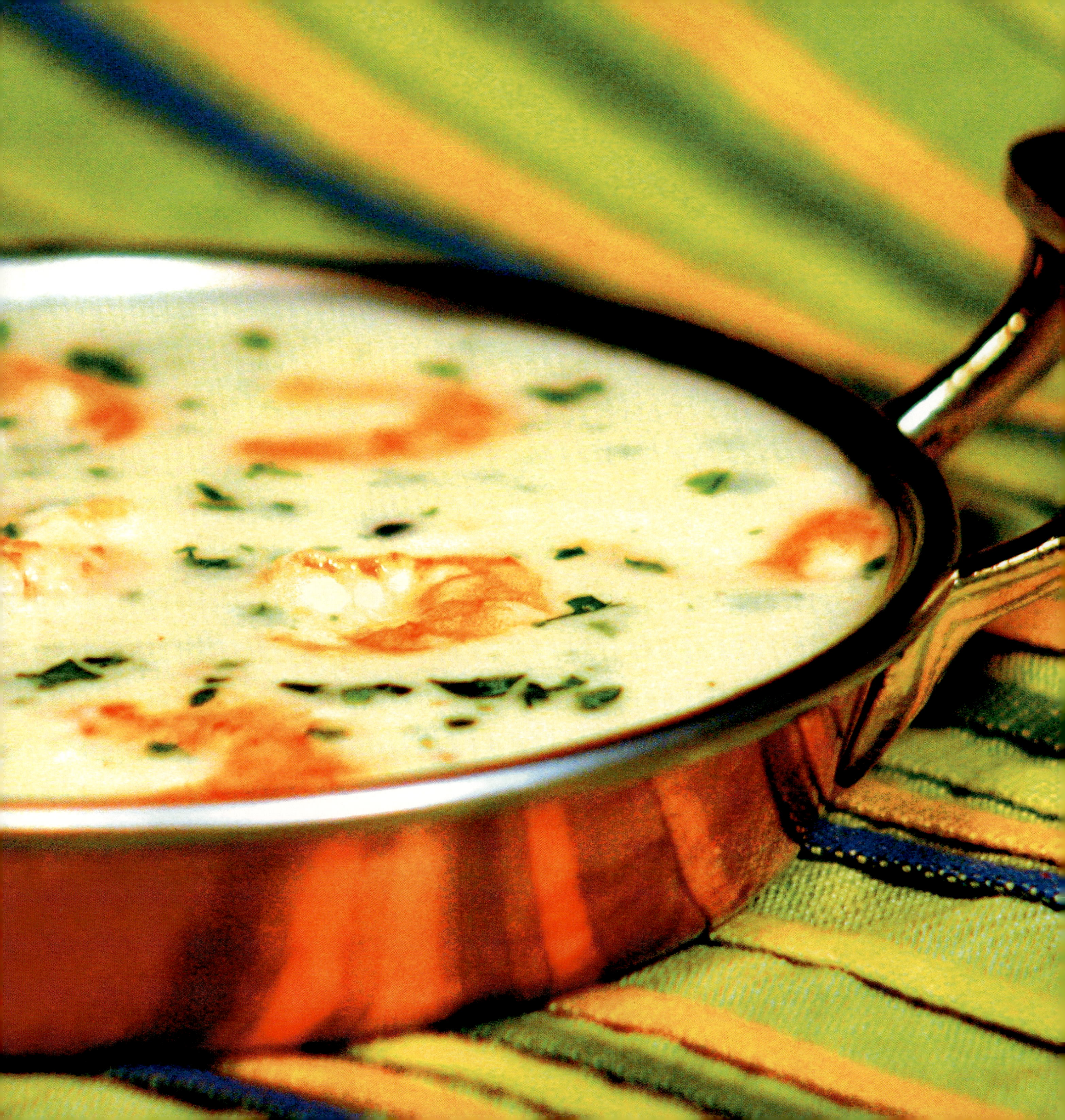

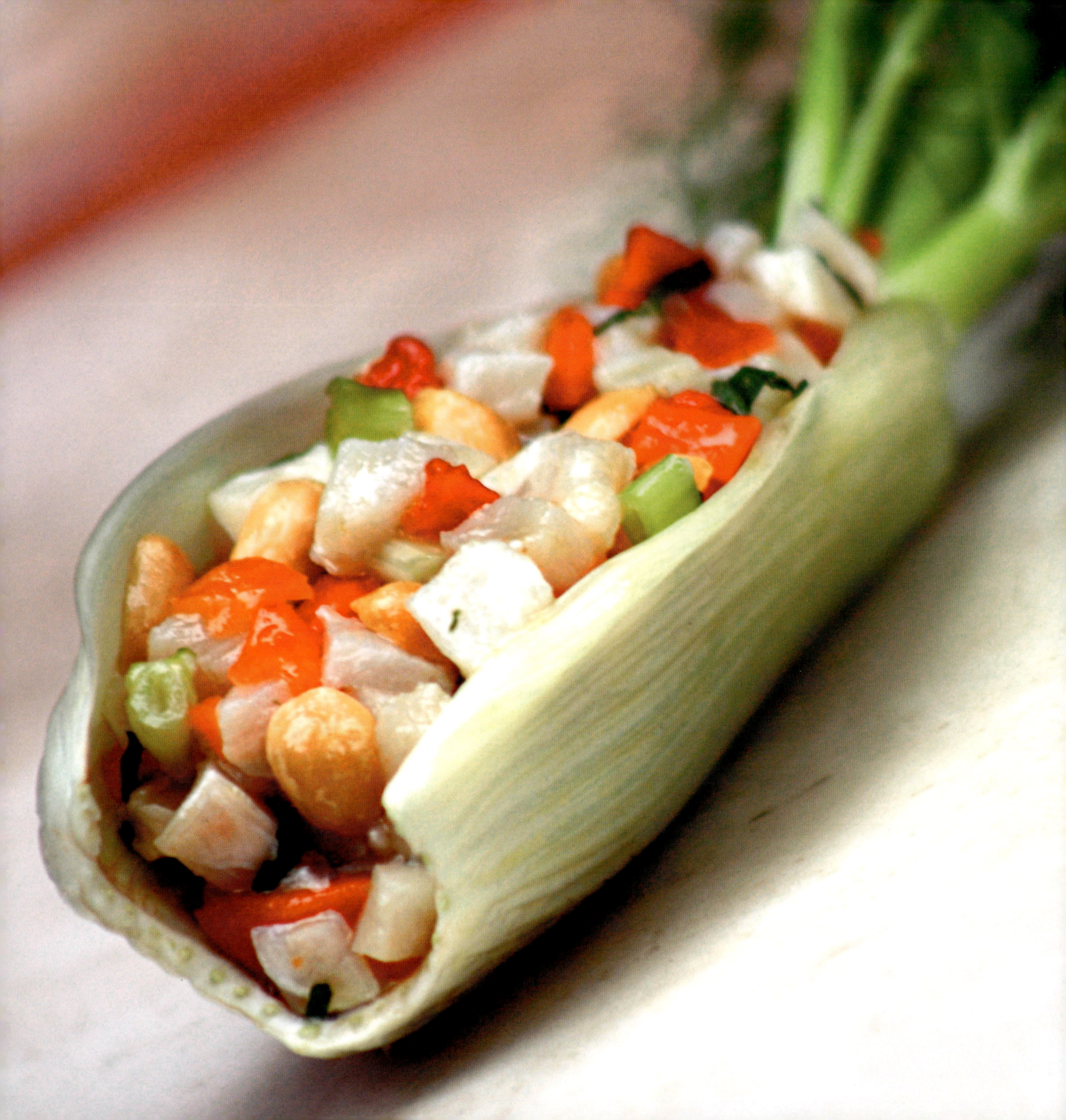

Snook salad
with papaya and peanuts

350 g snook, diced
juice of 1 lime
60 ml olive oil
140 g fennels
80 g crystallized papayas, chopped
mint to taste
peanuts to taste
salt and pepper to taste

♪ Preparation: cut snook in small cubes and season with lime, olive oil, salt and pepper. Marinate it for 30 minutes. Cut fennel stalks in half moons and set aside to serve with salad.

♪ To assemble: add the remaining ingredients, season to taste and mix with reserved stalks.

♪ Servings: 4 portions

♪ Preparation time: 30 minutes

Tepid calamari
salad

60 ml olive oil
20 g garlic, smashed
180 g cherry tomatoes, halved
400 g calamari rings
juice of 1 lemon
100 g rocket leaves, roughly chopped
salt and pepper to taste
parsley to taste

♪ Preparation: season calamari with 1 tablespoon olive oil, salt, pepper and lime and marinate for 10 minutes. In a skillet, fry garlic in remaining olive oil until golden brown. Add tomatoes and calamari and sauté slightly. Finally add rocket and remove from heat.

♪ To assemble: using a round mold, place salad in 4 dishes and serve.

♪ Servings: 4 portions

♪ Preparation time: 45 minutes

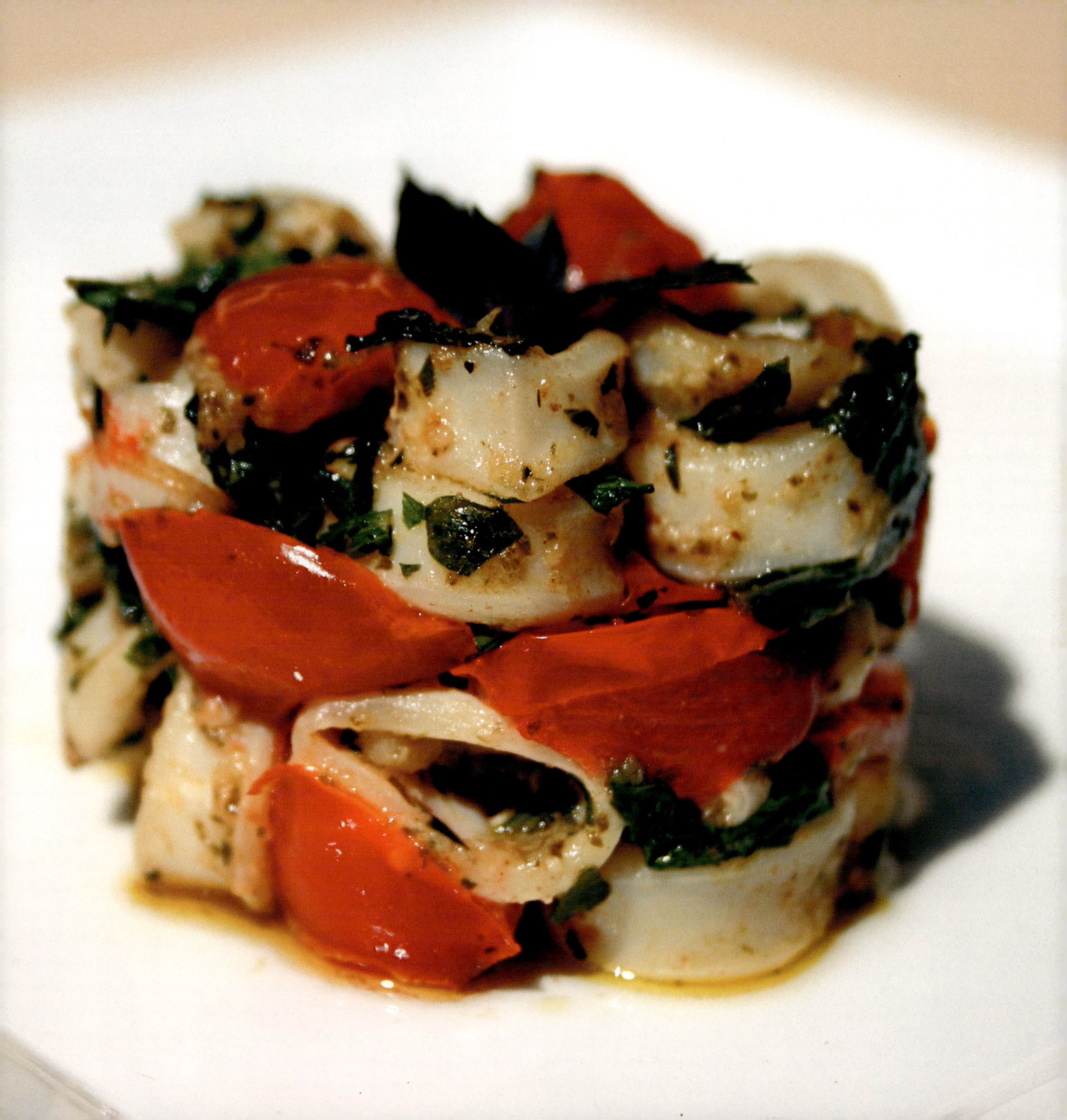

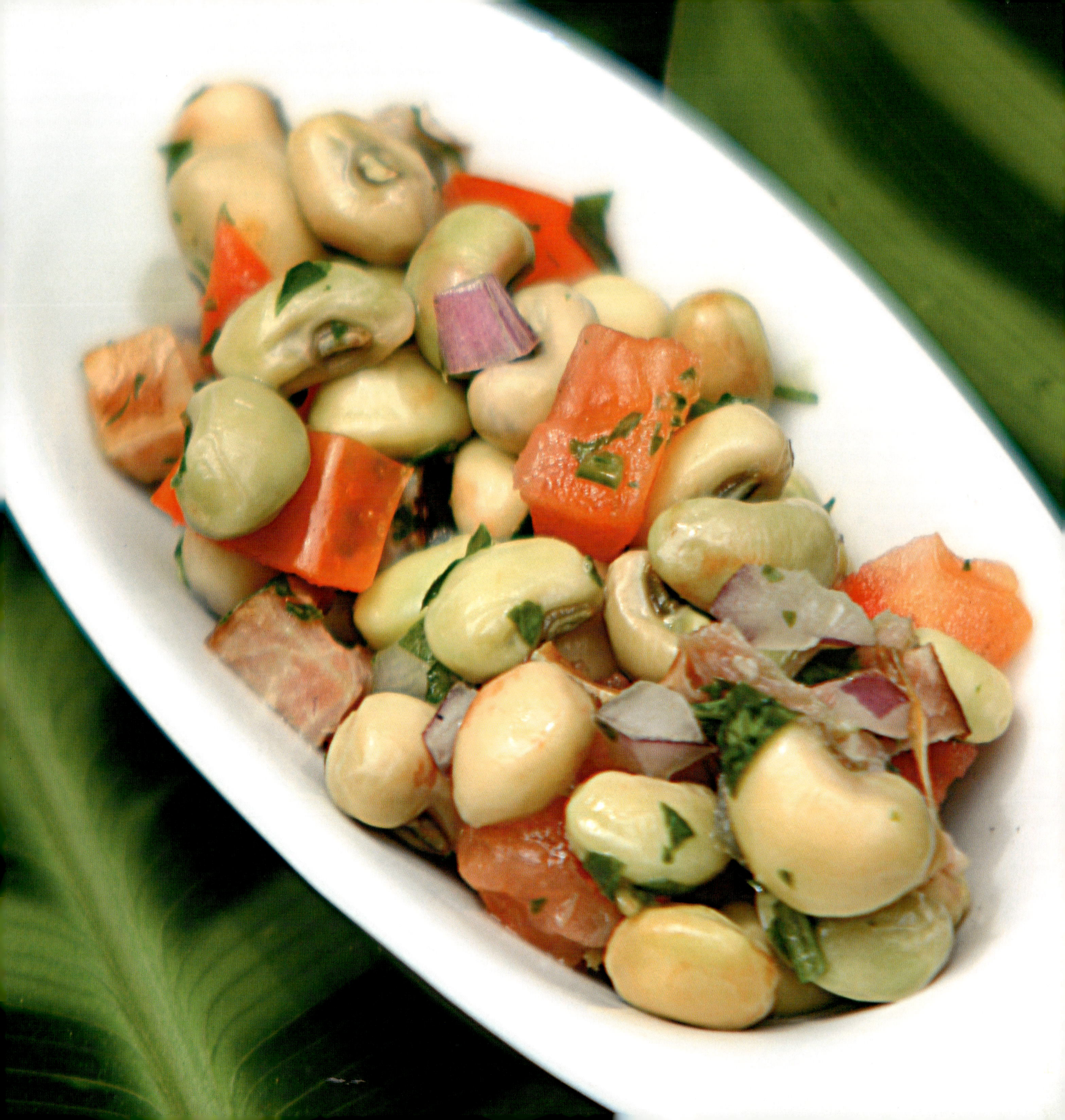

Beans, tomato
and red onion salad

600 g black-eyed beans
water and salt
10 g bacon
60 g clarified butter
400 g tomatoes
200 g red onions
1 lime
salt and pepper to taste
chopped parsley to taste

♪ Preparation: cook beans in water and salt until tender. Fry bacon in clarified butter. Set aside. Dice tomato and onion. Mix ingredients and season with lime, salt and pepper. Finally, sprinkle with chopped parsley.

♪ Servings: 4 portions

♪ Preparation time: 2 hours

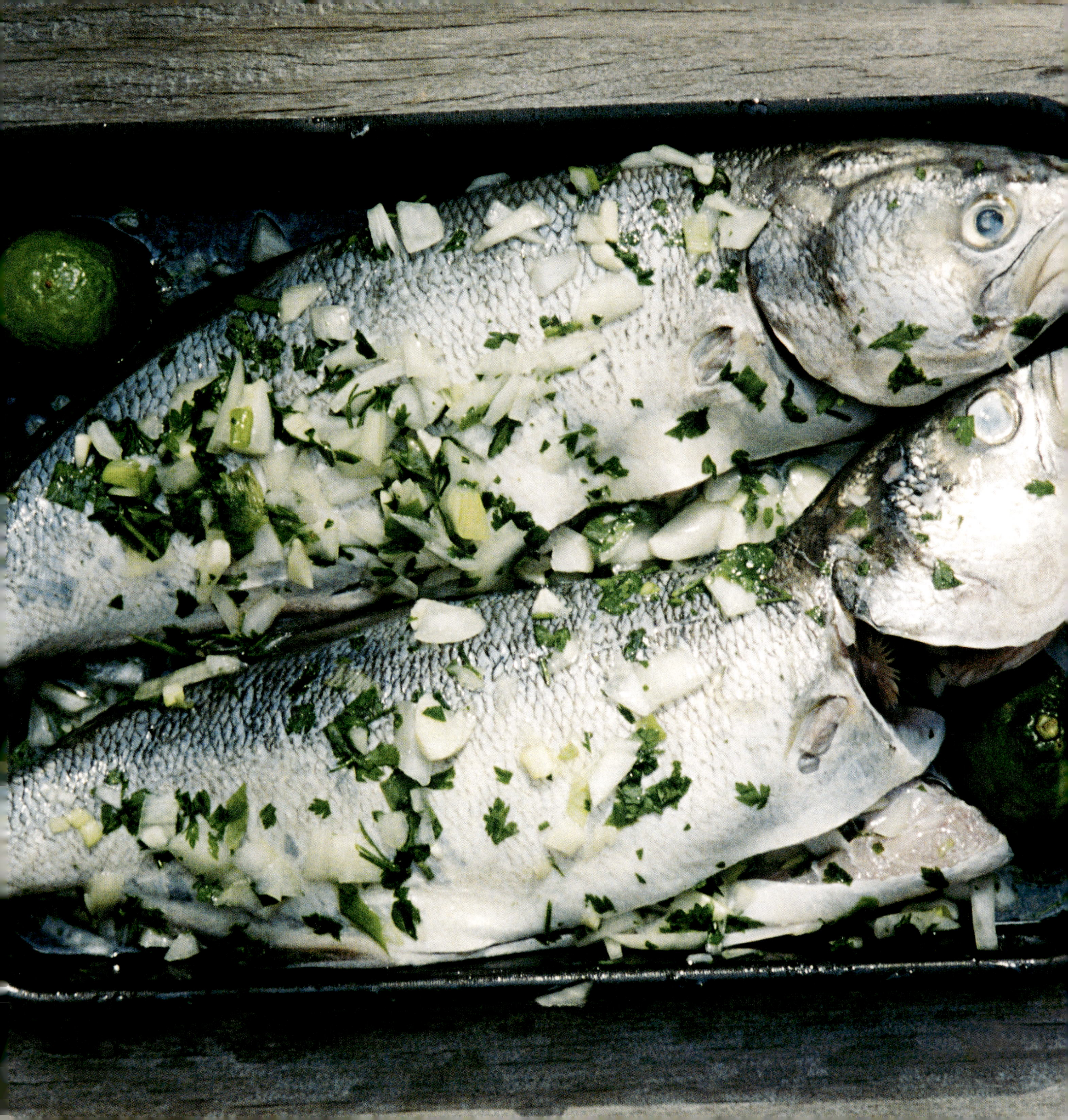

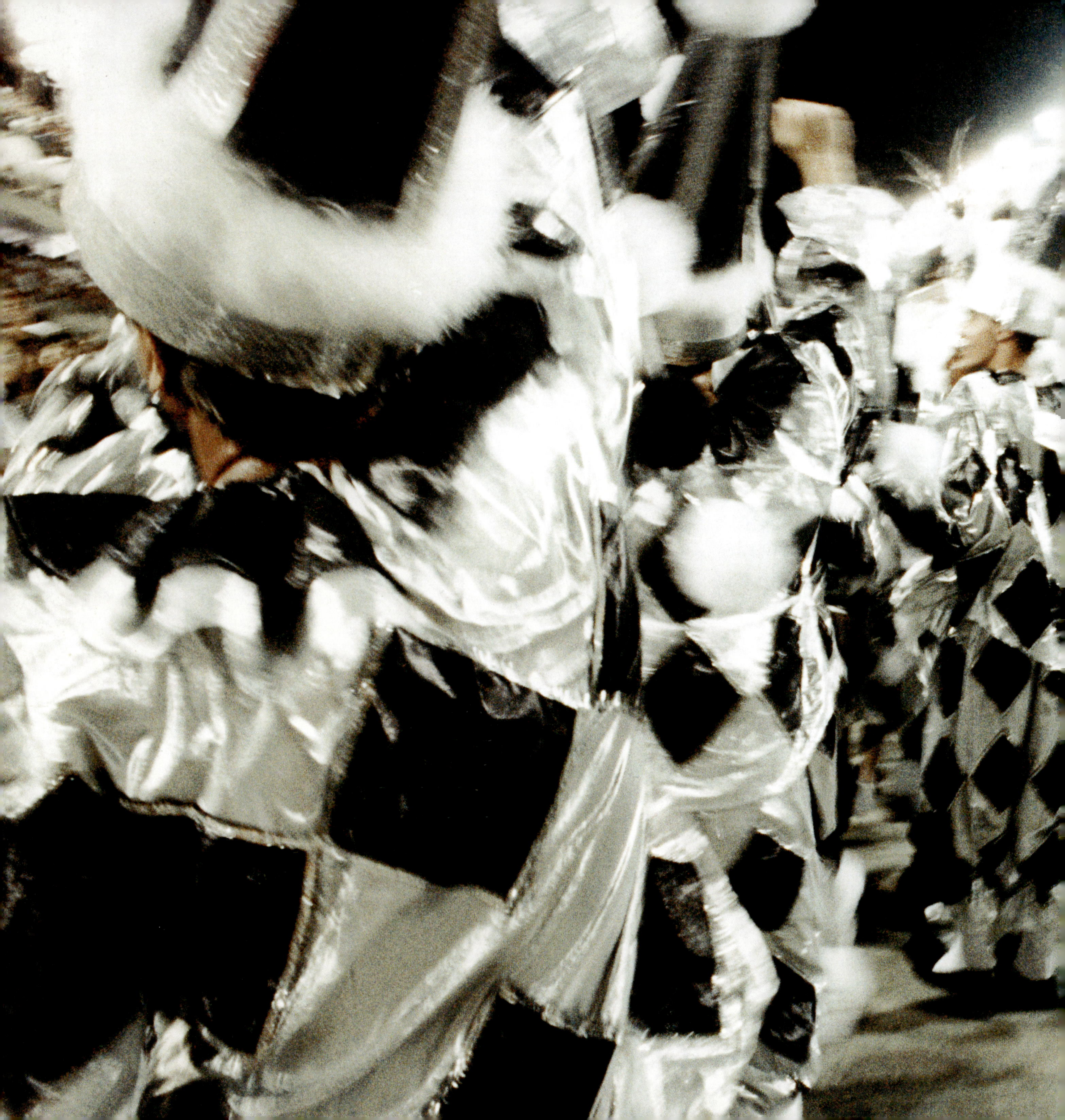

"No tabuleiro da baiana tem:
Vatapá, oi, carurú, mugunzá, tem umbu
Pra Ioiô
Se eu pedir você me dá o seu coração
Seu amor de Iaiá?"

♪ Ary Barroso, No tabuleiro da baiana

Stewed chicken : p.68
Chicken cake with requeijão cremoso : p.70
Sautéed tenderloin with banana farofa : p.72
Lamb loin roast with coffee sauce and cassava rösti : p.74
Feijoada : p.76
Rice and beans with jerked beef : p.78
Grilled tenderloin medallion with queijo coalho : p.80
Stuffed squash with jerked beef on bed of kale : p.82
Yellow yam gnocchi with watercress sauce : p.84
Capellini al mare : p.86
Grilled scallops with caipirinha risotto : p.88
Stuffed sea bass with shrimp farofa : p.90
Grilled flounder with pinyon and green salad : p.92
Roasted cod chunks : p.94
Snook with cashew nut crust : p.96
Seafood moqueca with coconut rice : p.98
Snook medallion with smoked catfish : p.100
Grilled langoustines with plantains : p.102
Crab frittata : p.104
Lobster grilled in pineapple : p.106
Shrimp stew with curry and coconut milk : p.108

ENTRÉES

Stewed chicken

1 whole chicken of about 2 kg
500 ml cachaça or light rum
2 limes
30 g urucum powder (tasteless red coloring)
300 g garlic, smashed
600 g onions, chopped
chopped cilantro to taste
100 ml dende oil (palm oil)

♪ Vegetables:
200 g pumpkins, diced
200 g yellow yam (mandioquinha), diced
200 g zucchinis, diced
200 g chayote, diced
200 g carrots, diced
salt and pepper to taste

♪ Preparation: cut chicken at joints and scald it (pour boiling water and then wash it with running water); season with salt and pepper and set aside. Prepare a marinade with limes, red coloring, garlic, onion and cilantro. Add to chicken and leave it overnight. Set aside marinade mixture. In a skillet, warm dende oil and fry chicken. Add marinade and cover with water. Cook for about 40 minutes. Remove chicken from liquid and add diced vegetables. Cook until soft. Season with salt and pepper.

♪ Servings: 10 portions

♪ Preparation time: one day

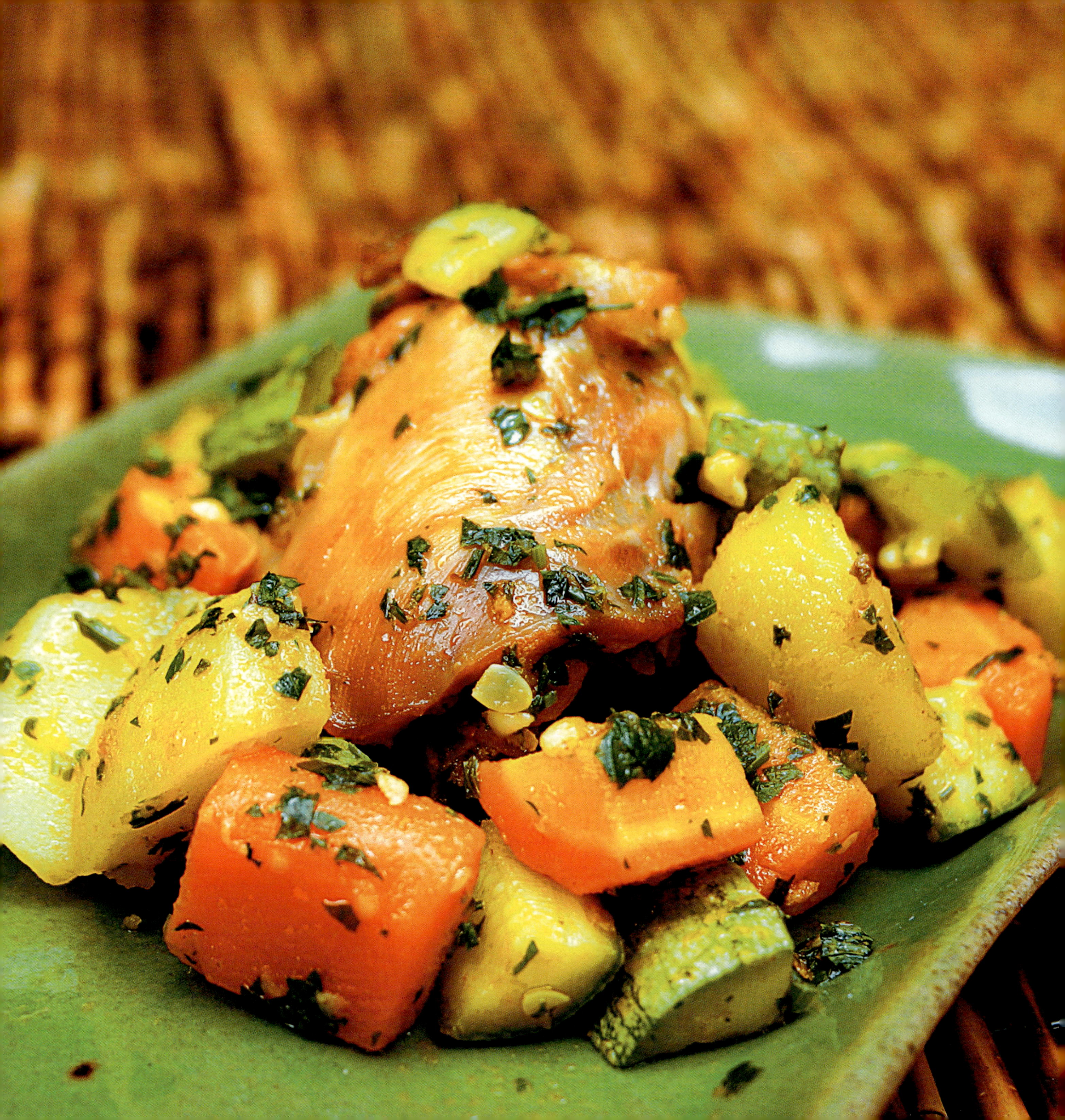

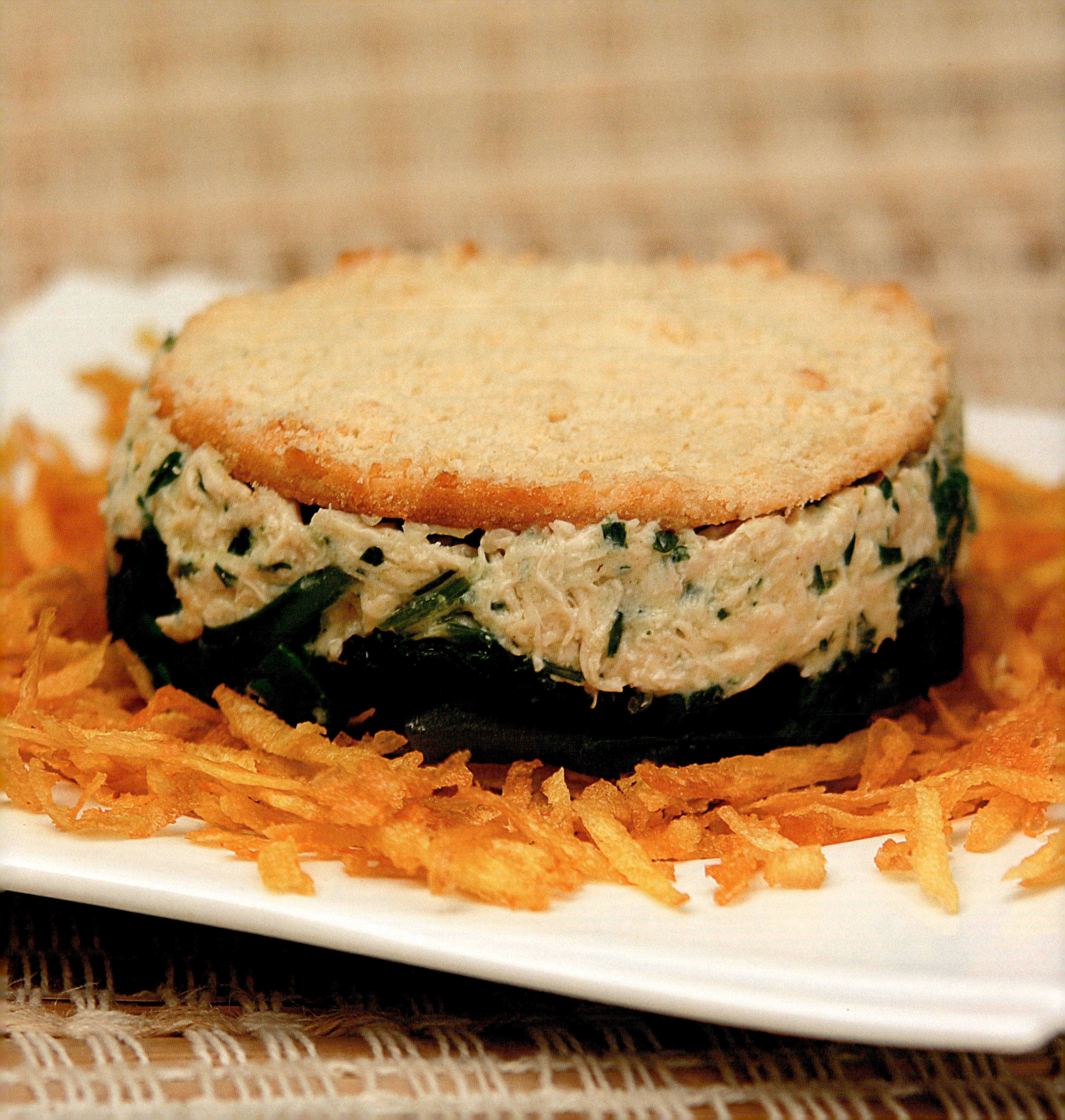

Chicken cake with *requeijão cremoso*, sautéed spinach and grated yellow yam

♪ Chicken:
800 g chicken breast / water and salt, to cook / 50 g butter
2 garlic cloves, smashed / 1 onion, finely chopped / basil to taste
200 g **requeijão** cremoso or buttermilk cheese / 600 *ml* milk / salt and pepper to taste

♪ Preparation: cook chicken breast in water and salt, until meat is tender and white. Remove from heat, rinse to eliminate odor, leave it to cool. Shred chicken with your hands. In a skillet, melt butter and sauté garlic until golden brown; add onion and sauté for some minutes. Add shredded chicken and basil leaves. Pour milk and buttermilk cheese. Season with salt and pepper. Cook until it thickens.

♪ Sautéed spinach: 1 kg spinachs / 12 garlic cloves, smashed / 100 *ml* olive oil / salt and pepper to taste

♪ Preparation: in a skillet, heat oil and sauté garlic until golden brown. Add spinach and cook until wilted and reduced to half the size.

♪ Grated yellow yam: 400 g yellow yam, thickly grated / oil, for frying

♪ Preparation: grate yams and rinse. Fry in very hot oil until they are golden and crunchy.

♪ Topping (*farofa*): 800 g flour / 400 g butter / salt and pepper, to taste

♪ Preparation: mix flour and butter with your fingers until you obtain a coarse meal. Season with salt and pepper to taste.

♪ To assemble: this dish can be assembled in two ways: 1. Place spinach as a base, then top it with chicken and then the farofa, either in a serving dish or in four individual ramekins. Bake in medium heat, until topping is golden. Serve grated yam as a side dish. 2. Divide the farofa into four portions; using a round mold, form four disks and bake them on a baking sheet lined with parchment paper. Then assemble dish using the mold: one layer of spinach, one layer of sautéed chicken and, finally, the roasted *farofa* disk. Serve grated yam around the disk.

♪ Servings: 4 portions

♪ Preparation time: 1 hour

Sautéed tenderloin
with banana *farofa*

800 g tenderloin, diced
60 g butter
20 g garlic, smashed
300 g onions
salt and pepper to taste
350 ml beef broth (optional)
150 ml dark beer
parsley to taste

♪ **Preparation:** sauté garlic and onion in butter. Add diced beef. Sauté until golden and liquid is reduced. Season with salt and pepper. Pour beef broth and beer, simmer to reduce liquid. Add chopped parsley.

♪ **Banana *farofa*:** 150 g butter / 2 small bananas, sliced / 600 g cassava flour / salt and pepper to taste / parsley to taste

♪ **Preparation:** sauté cassava flour and half the butter for a few minutes. In a saucepan, sauté the banana and the rest of the butter. Add mixture to the farofa. Season with parsley, salt and pepper.

♪ **Fried quail eggs:** 30 g butter / 8 quail eggs / salt to taste

♪ **Preparation:** fry eggs in butter and season with salt.

♪ **To assemble:** place a portion of sautéed sirloin on the plate between two fried quail eggs. Top it with the banana farofa.

♪ **Servings:** 4 portions

♪ **Preparation time:** 45 minutes

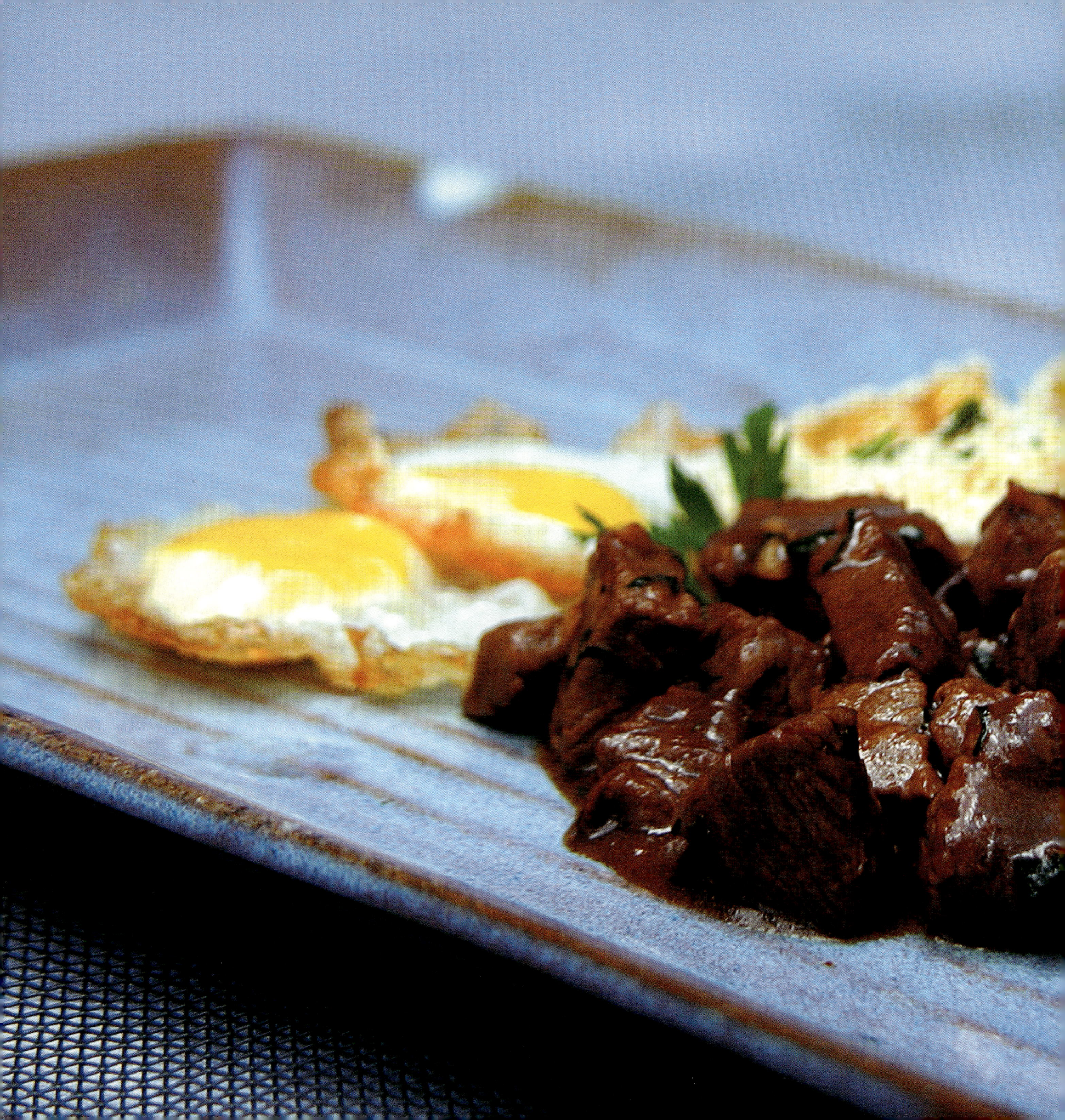

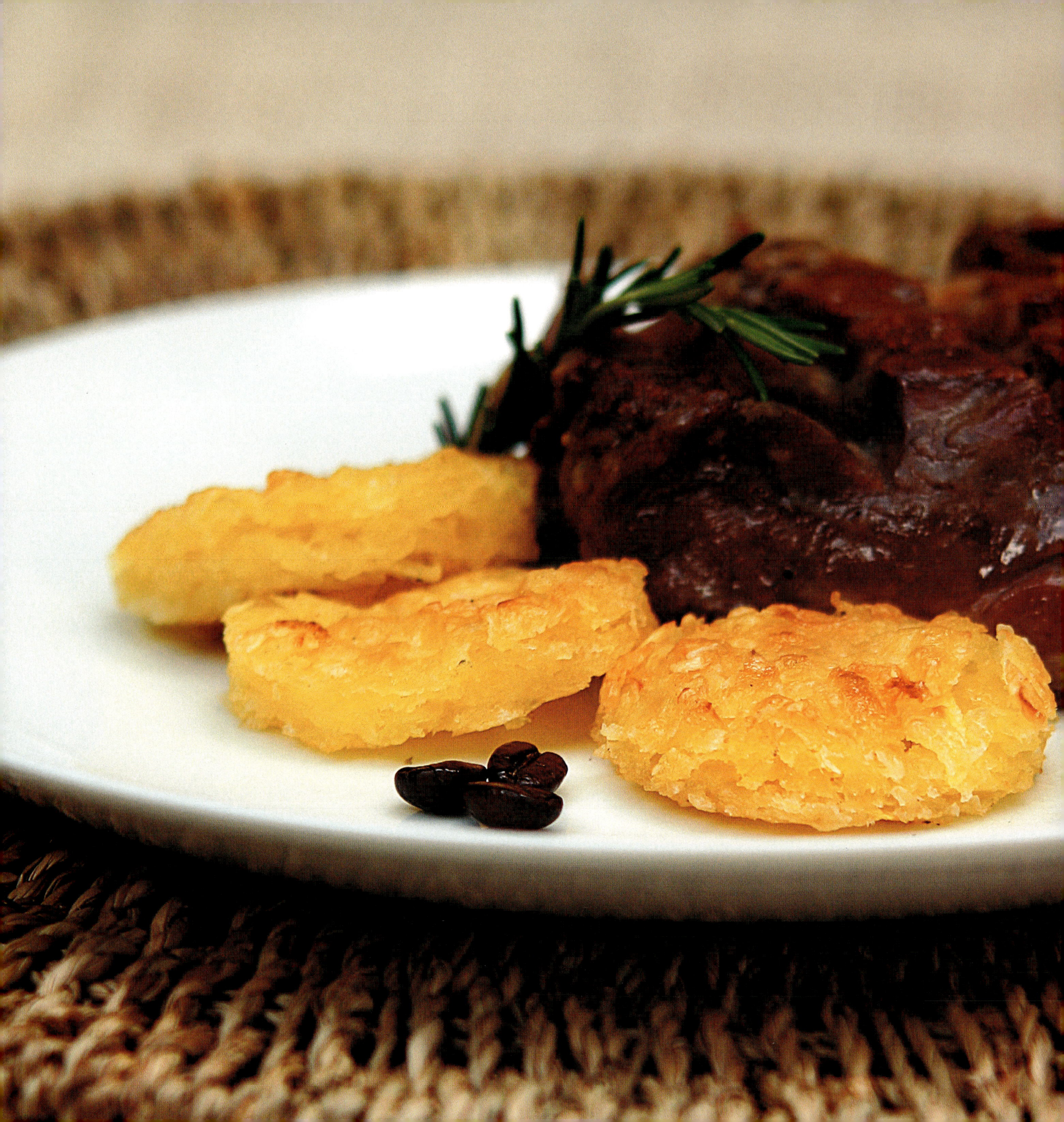

Lamb loin roast with coffee sauce
and cassava Rösti

♪ Lamb:
1 kg lamb loin roast
salt and pepper to taste
rosemary, to taste
120 ml olive oil

♪ Preparation: season meat with salt, pepper and rosemary. Roast it with olive oil until tender.

♪ Coffee sauce: 300 ml beef broth / 50 ml (mild) coffee / 30 g honey / salt and pepper to taste

♪ Preparation: in a saucepan, simmer broth and coffee until reduced. Season with honey, salt and pepper.

♪ Cassava Rösti: 600 g cassava, grated / 200 g soft-ripened cheese, grated / salt and pepper to taste / 100 g butter, melted

♪ Preparation: mix grated cassava and cheese, season with salt and pepper; add butter until a dough is formed. Roll dough out on a clean surface and, using a cookie cutter or a glass, cut eight circles. Place them on a baking sheet and place it in preheated oven for 20 minutes.

♪ To assemble: place lamb on a plate, cover it with coffee sauce, garnish with a sprig of rosemary. Serve with röstis. If prefered, serve coffee sauce separately.

♪ Servings: 4 portions

♪ Preparation time: 45 minutes

Feijoada

(This is a very traditional Brazilian stew prepared with black beans and pork)

1 kg black beans
500 g jerked beef, diced
200 g salted bacon slab
150 g smoked pork loin, diced
150 g pork ribs
1 onion
1 celery
2 bay leaves
1/2 orange
100 g bacon, diced
150 g paio
150 g Calabrese sausage, sliced
oil, for frying
2 onions, finely chopped
4 garlic cloves, smashed
50 *ml* cachaça or light rum
1 red hot chili pepper
salt to taste
chopped parsley to taste

♪ Preparation: the day before, wash beans and leave them in water overnight. Rinse jerked beef, bacon slabs, pork loin and ribs. Leave them in water overnight. The following day, change beans water and cook them with the whole onion, whole celery, bay leaves and the orange. Cover with lid and cook until beans are soft, adding more water if necessary. Rinse meat once again. Cook them in separate saucepans, since every meat has its own cooking time. Once cooked, add all meat and its broth to beans. Fry diced bacon in a litlle oil and add to beans. In a skillet, fry sausages and add to beans. Prepare seasoning: sauté garlic and onion in oil, until brown, plus one cup beans, the cachaça and the chili pepper. Blend. Pour mixture into the beans pan and check seasoning; if necessary, add more salt or pepper. If meat is not well cooked, add more water and cook until tender. If the *feijoada* is too thin, blend another cup of cooked beans and add it to the *feijoada*. Remove orange, celery and onion. Add chopped parsley and serve.

♪ Suggestion: serve *feijoada* with sautéed kale, cassava *farofa*, crumbed banana, sliced oranges and crackling.

♪ Servings: 10 portions

♪ Preparation time: 2 days

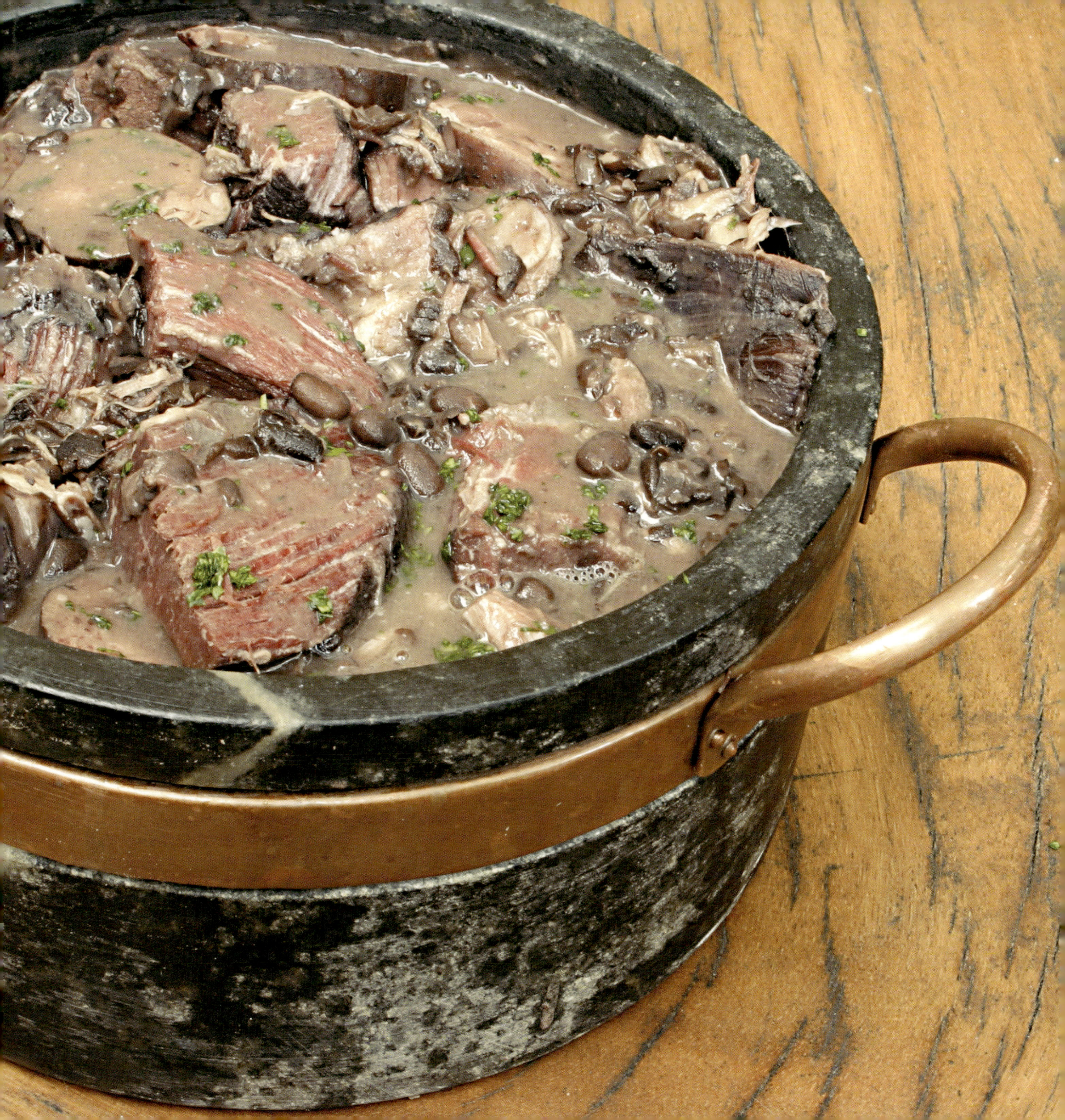

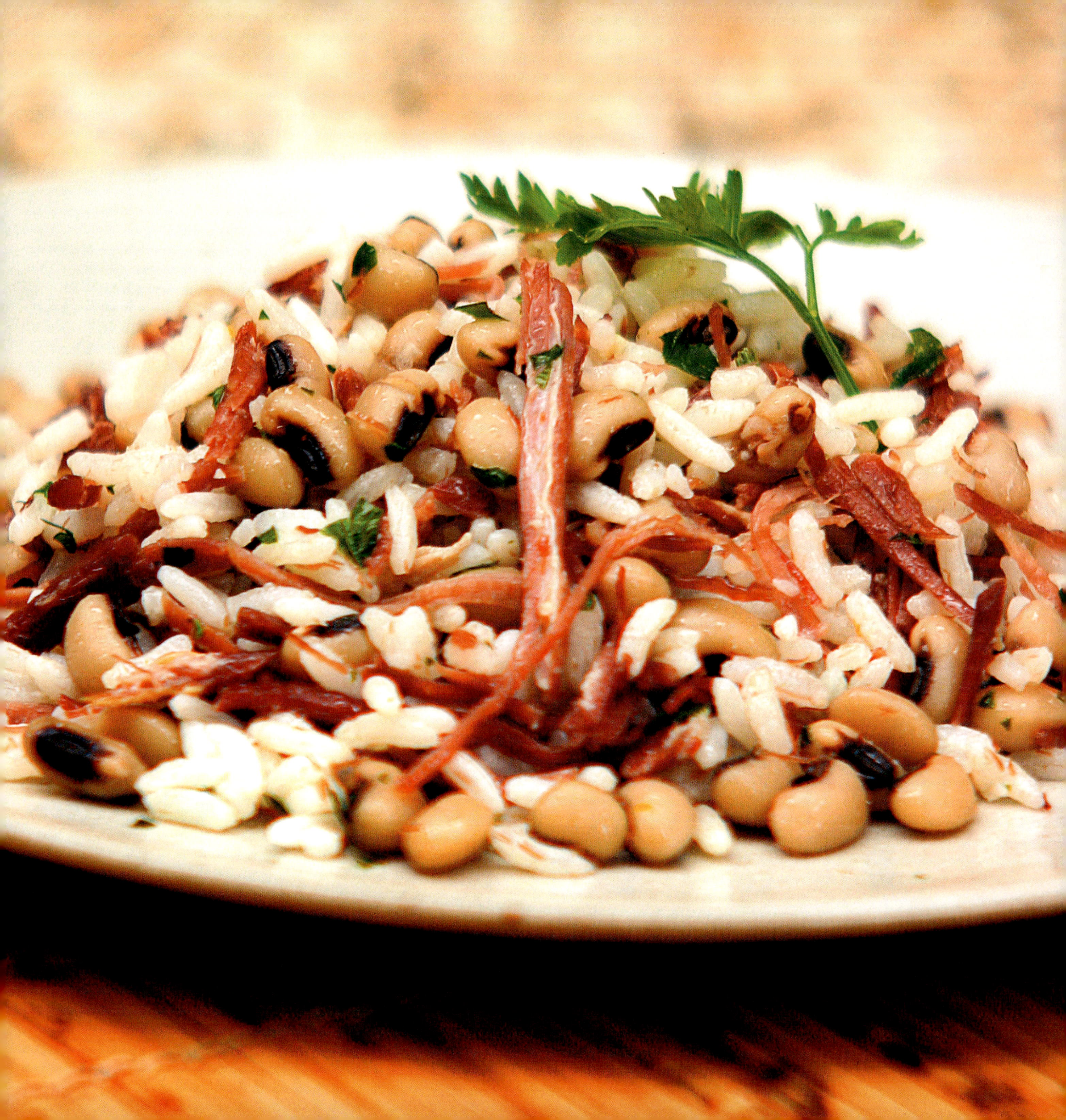

Rice and beans
with jerked beef

250 g jerked beef, diced
300 g black-eyed beans
1 bay leaf
100 g salted slab bacon, chopped
30 g garlic, smashed
300 g onions, diced
2 tomatoes, diced
parsley to taste
salt and pepper to taste
300 g cooked rice

♪ Preparation: leave jerked beef in water overnight. Cook it changing its water after it had boiled (repeat procedure 3 times). Remove fat, shred and reserve it. Cook beans in water, salt and bay leaf, until soft; drain water and set aside. Fry slabs in its own fat and, in the same saucepan, sauté garlic and onion. Add jerked beef, tomato, parsley, salt and pepper. Transfer this mixture to beans and add previously cooked rice. Serve it in the saucepan or in a serving dish.

♪ Servings: 4 portions

♪ Preparation time: 2 days

Grilled tenderloin medallion with *queijo coalho* and sugarcane syrup

♪ Grilled medallion:
1 kg tenderloin (8 medallions)
100 ml olive oil
salt and pepper to taste
200 g **queijo coalho** *or curd cheese*

♪ Preparation: season medallions with salt and pepper. Heat a skillet with oil until hot. Then add medallions and grill for 2 minutes each side. Remove from skillet and set aside. Finish cooking in the oven for 5 minutes, before serving.

♪ Sugarcane syrup sauce: 100 ml sugarcane syrup / 600 ml beef broth

♪ Preparation: in the same skillet used for medallions, add syrup and broth. Stir with a wooden spoon to loosen any particles in the bottom of the pan so as to add them to the sauce. Simmer until reduced and thickened. Set aside.

♪ Grilled curd cheese: 200 g curd cheese

♪ Preparation: cut two medium slices of curd cheese. In a skillet, add a little oil and grill cheese on both sides. Set aside.

♪ Sautéed heart of palms: 400 g fresh heart of palms / water to cook / 100 ml olive oil / salt and pepper to taste / parsley to taste

♪ Preparation: cook heart of palms in water and salt. Once tender, remove from heat and leave it to cool. Cut it in thin slices and sauté them in olive oil with salt and pepper. Sprinkle parsley.

♪ To assemble: transfer medallions to individual plates and top them with grilled cheese and then the syrup. Garnish with sautéed heart of palms.

♪ Servings: 4 portions

♪ Preparation time: 1 hour

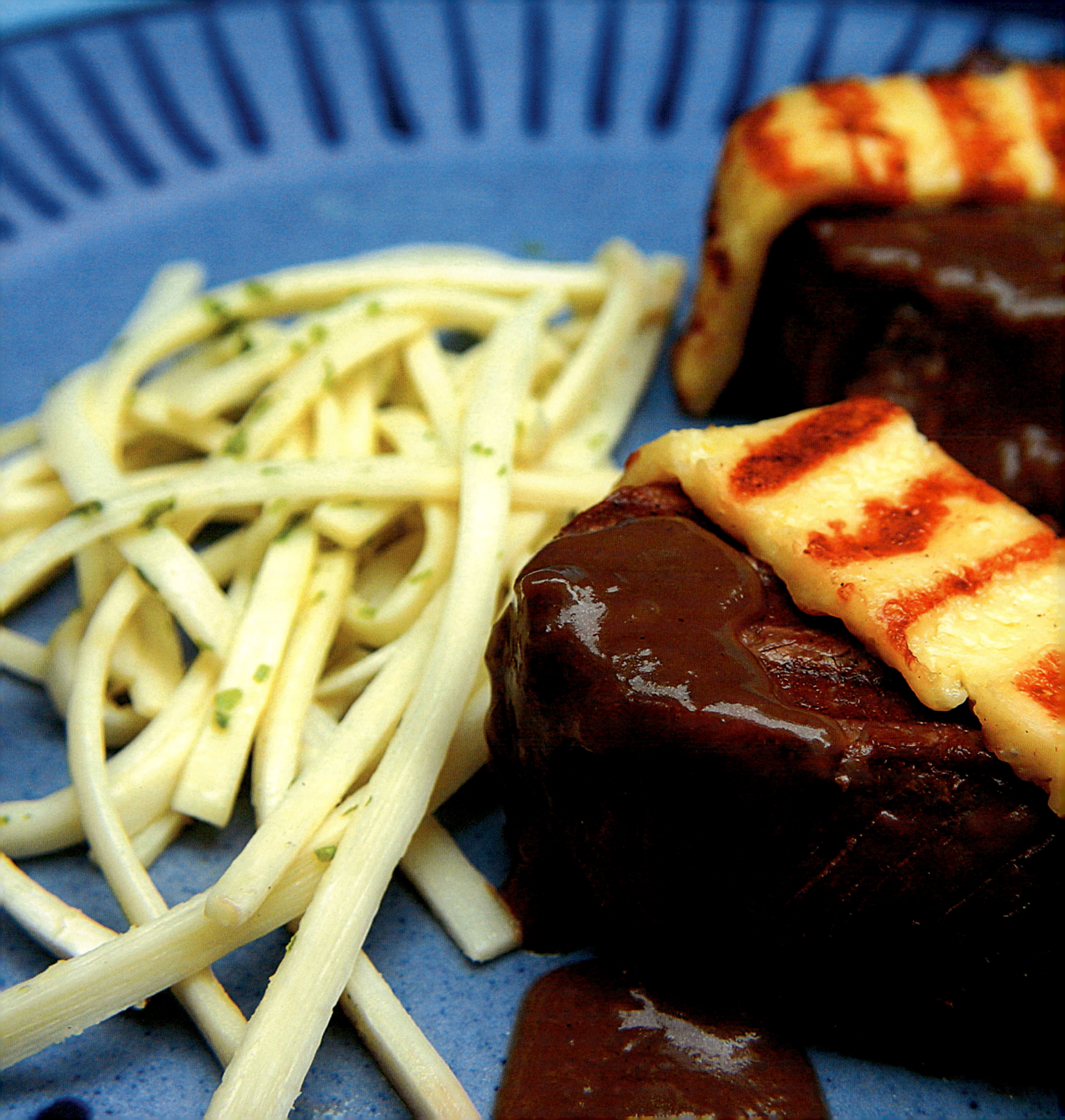

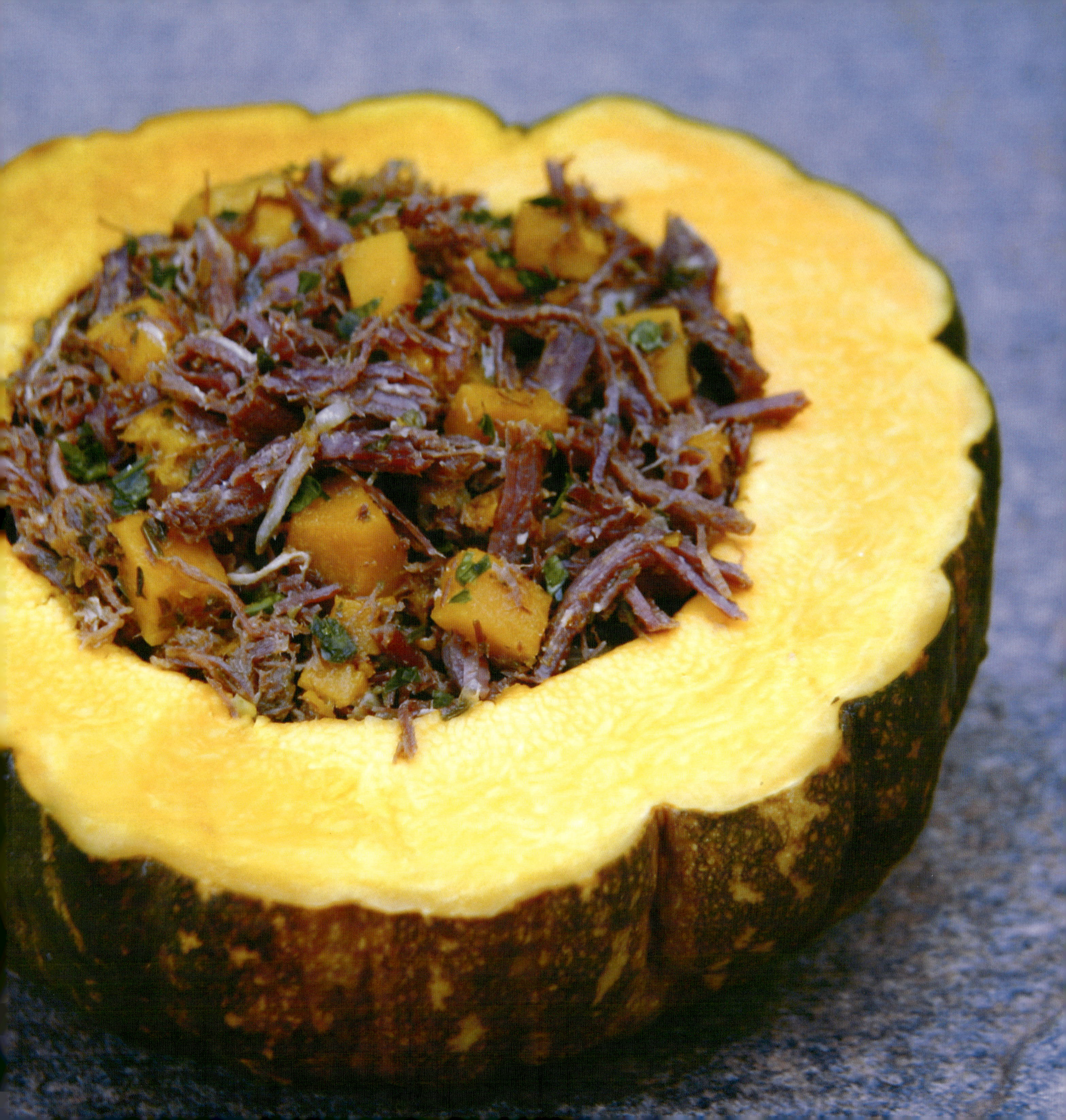

Stuffed squash
with jerked beef on bed of kale

4 small, whole kabocha squash (Japanese squash)
800 g jerked beef
200 ml clarified butter
400 g onions, chopped
60 g garlic
parsley to taste

♪ Preparation: cut squashes into halves, set aside 4 halves to sauté and cook the other four *al dente*. Desalt the jerked beef in a bowl with plenty of water, changing the water every hour for 4 hours. Cook jerked beef in a pressure cooker with water for 30 minutes until tender and roughly shred it with your hands. Dice (in medium cubes) half of the remaining squash. Put part of the clarified butter in a skillet and sauté the squash until tender. Set aside. Fry garlic with the remaining clarified butter. Add sliced onion and shredded jerked beef and plenty of parsley. Taste to adjust seasoning. Place squash into the skillet with the sautéed beef and mix well. Stuff the squash with this mixture.

♪ Sautéed kale: 800 g kale / 20 g garlic / 60 ml olive oil / salt and pepper to taste

♪ Preparation: thinly slice kale leaves. Fry garlic in olive oil until golden brown. Add kale and sauté until wilted. Season with salt and pepper.

♪ To assemble: on an individual plate, toss kale and top it with stuffed squash.

♪ Servings: 4 portions

♪ Preparation time: 5 hours

Yellow yam gnocchi
with watercress sauce

800 g yellow yam
150 g all-purpose flour
30 g butter
1 egg
salt and pepper

♪ Preparation: boil yams in water and salt. Once cooked, peel yams and place them in the oven for 3 minutes to remove humidity. Mash yams and add remaining ingredients, mix well and divide dough into small balls. Boil them in water and salt, drain them in cold water to stop cooking process. Set aside.

♪ Watercress sauce: 1 bunch watercress, chopped / 100 g onions, chopped / 2g garlic, smashed / 30 *ml* olive oil / 300 *ml* cream / salt and pepper to taste

♪ Preparation: sauté the garlic and onion in olive oil until golden brown. Add watercress and heavy cream. Simmer and let it reduce for a few minutes. Season with salt and pepper. Blend in an electric blender or food processor and set aside.

♪ To assemble: serve gnocchi with watercress sauce on top.

♪ Servings: 4 portions

♪ Preparation time: 2 hours

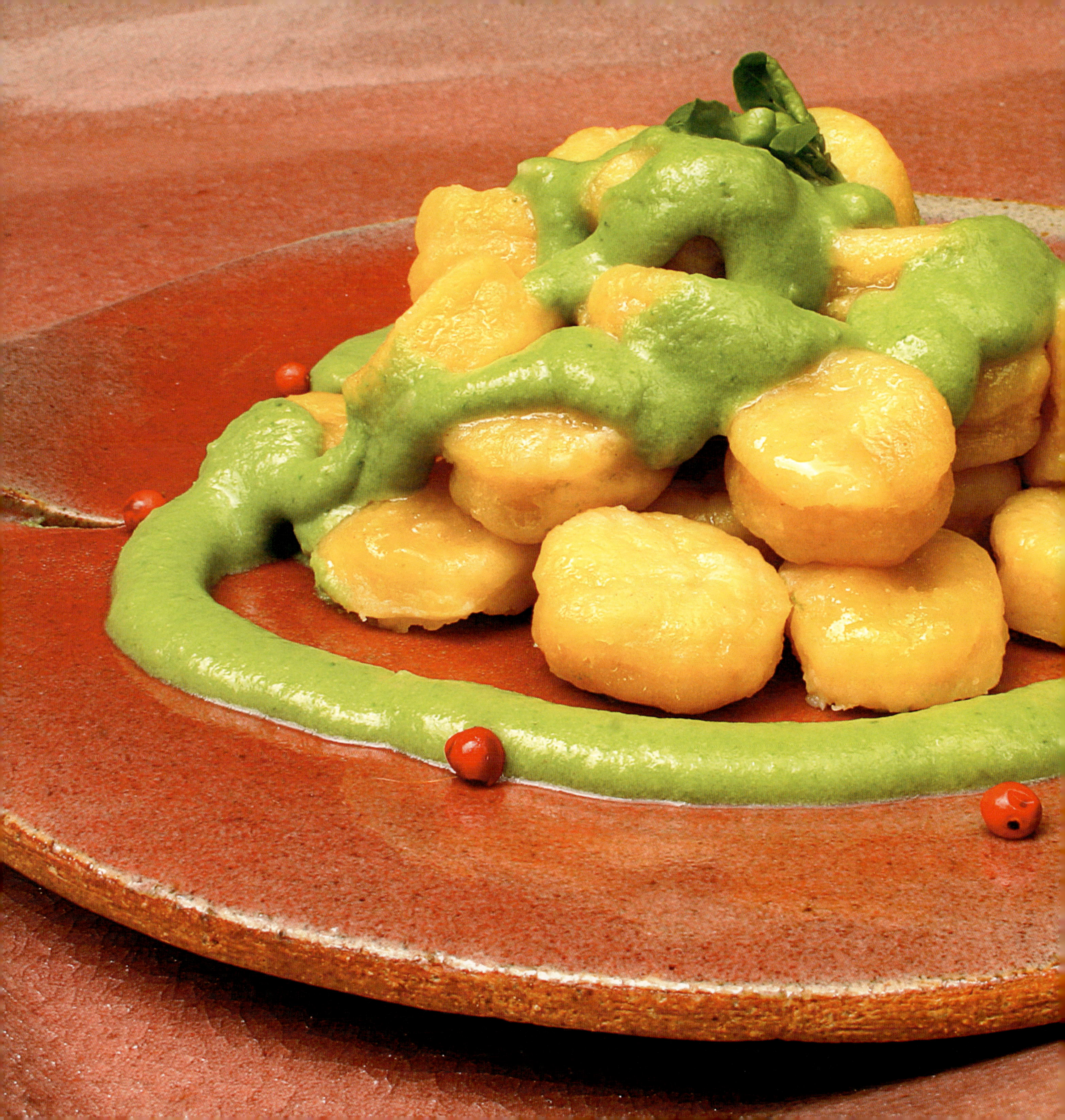

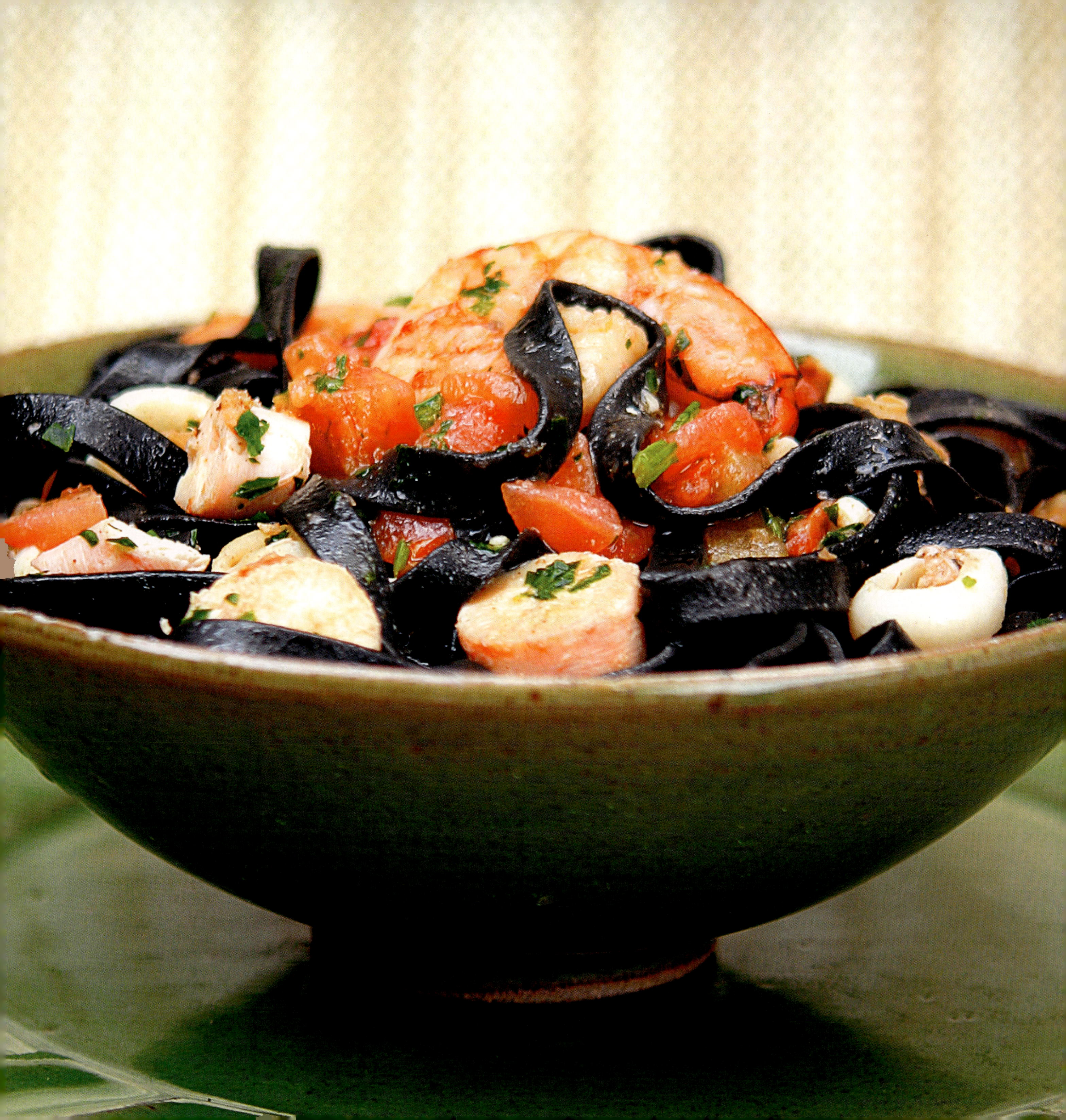

Capellini al mare
WITH SHRIMP, SQUID, MUSSEL, VONGOLE, TOMATO AND FRESH HERB SAUCE

♪ Capellini:
600 g all-purpose flour
6 eggs
32 ml squid ink (8 sacks)
10 ml olive oil
25 g salt

♪ Preparation: mix eggs, squid ink, olive oil and salt. Gradually add all-purpose flour and knead dough until smooth. Flatten dough with rolling pin. Cut into capellini shape and let it dry for a couple of hours.

♪ Sauce: 30 ml olive oil / 20 g garlic, smashed / 150 g shrimps / 150 g calamari / 50 g mussels / 50 g vongoli / 500 ml white wine / 200 g tomatoes, peeled / 200 g tomatoes, chopped / juice of 2 lemons / salt and pepper to taste / parsley to taste / basil to taste

♪ Preparation: brown garlic in olive oil. Add shrimps and let them brown. Add remaining seafood and sauté for a few minutes. Add wine, peeled and chopped tomatoes and lemon juice. Season with salt and pepper. Add parsley and basil.

♪ To assemble: cook pasta in water with salt and 1 spoon olive oil until *al dente*. Strain it and transfer to cold water to stop cooking process. Add sauce to pasta and serve.

♪ Servings: 4 portions

♪ Preparation time: 3 hours

Grilled scallops
with caipirinha risotto

800 g scallops (without shell)
juice of 1 lemon
salt and pepper to taste
100 ml olive oil

♪ Preparation: season scallops with lemon, salt and pepper, and set aside. Heat a skillet with olive oil until very hot and grill scallops.

♪ *Caipirinha* Risotto: 2 l vegetable broth / 1 onion, chopped / 60 g unsalted butter / 240 g arborio rice / 120 ml *cachaça* or light rum / lemon / salt and pepper to taste

♪ Preparation: boil vegetable broth in a saucepan with 500 ml water. When boiling, reduce heat. Sauté onion with one spoon of butter. Add rice and let it cook for about 2 minutes, stirring constantly. Add *cachaça* or light rum and stir until it evaporates. Add a ladle of vegetable broth (which must be very hot) and stir well. When broth has been absorbed, add one more ladle and repeat it until all broth has been absorbed, for around 15 minutes. Check its texture. If it is too *al dente* add some water. Once in the desired consistency, add juice and grated lemon zest. Turn off the heat and add another spoon of butter.

♪ To assemble: place risotto on a serving dish or on individual plates, top it with scallops and garnish with lemon slices.

♪ Servings: 4 people

♪ Preparation time: 1 hour

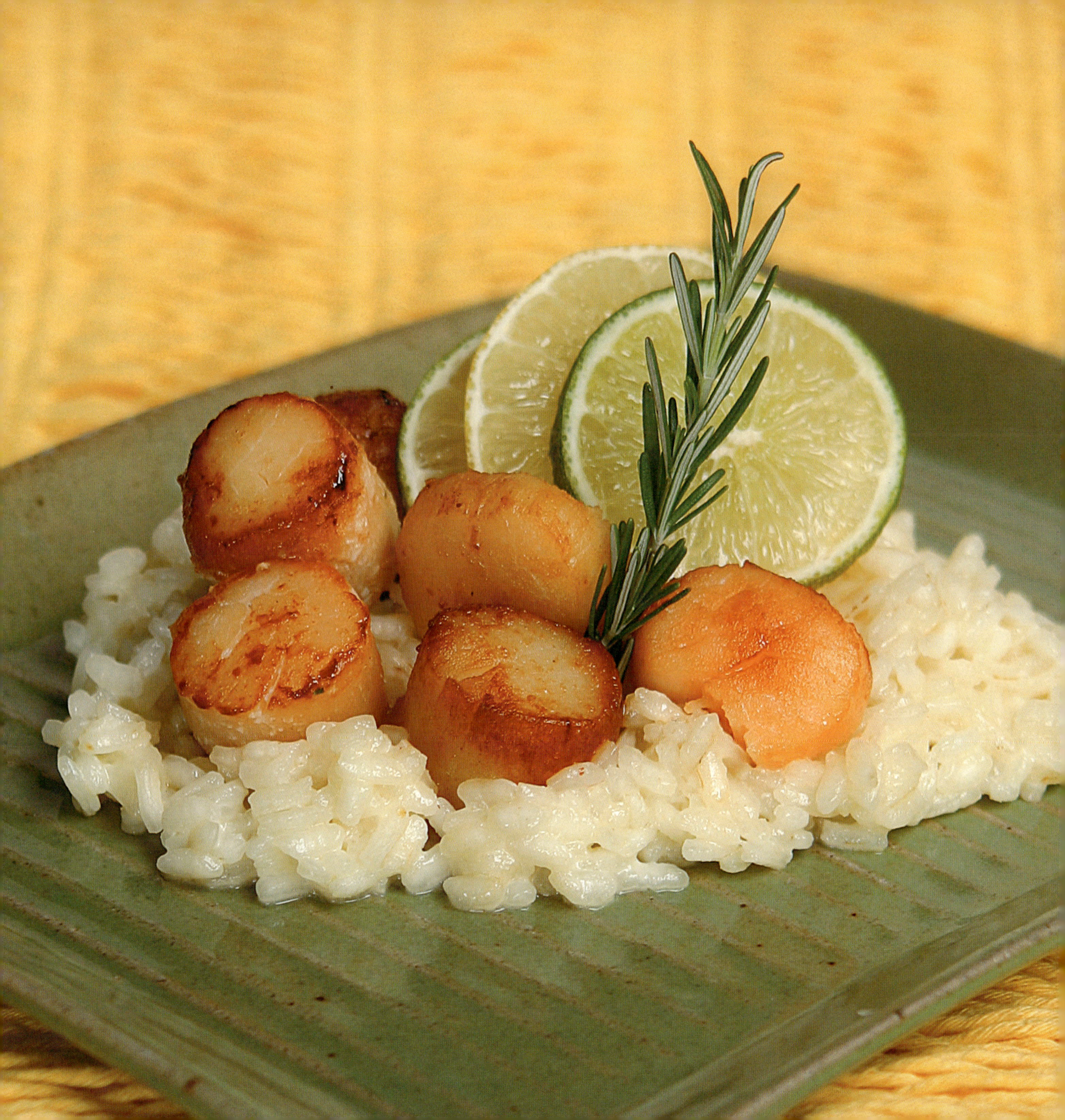

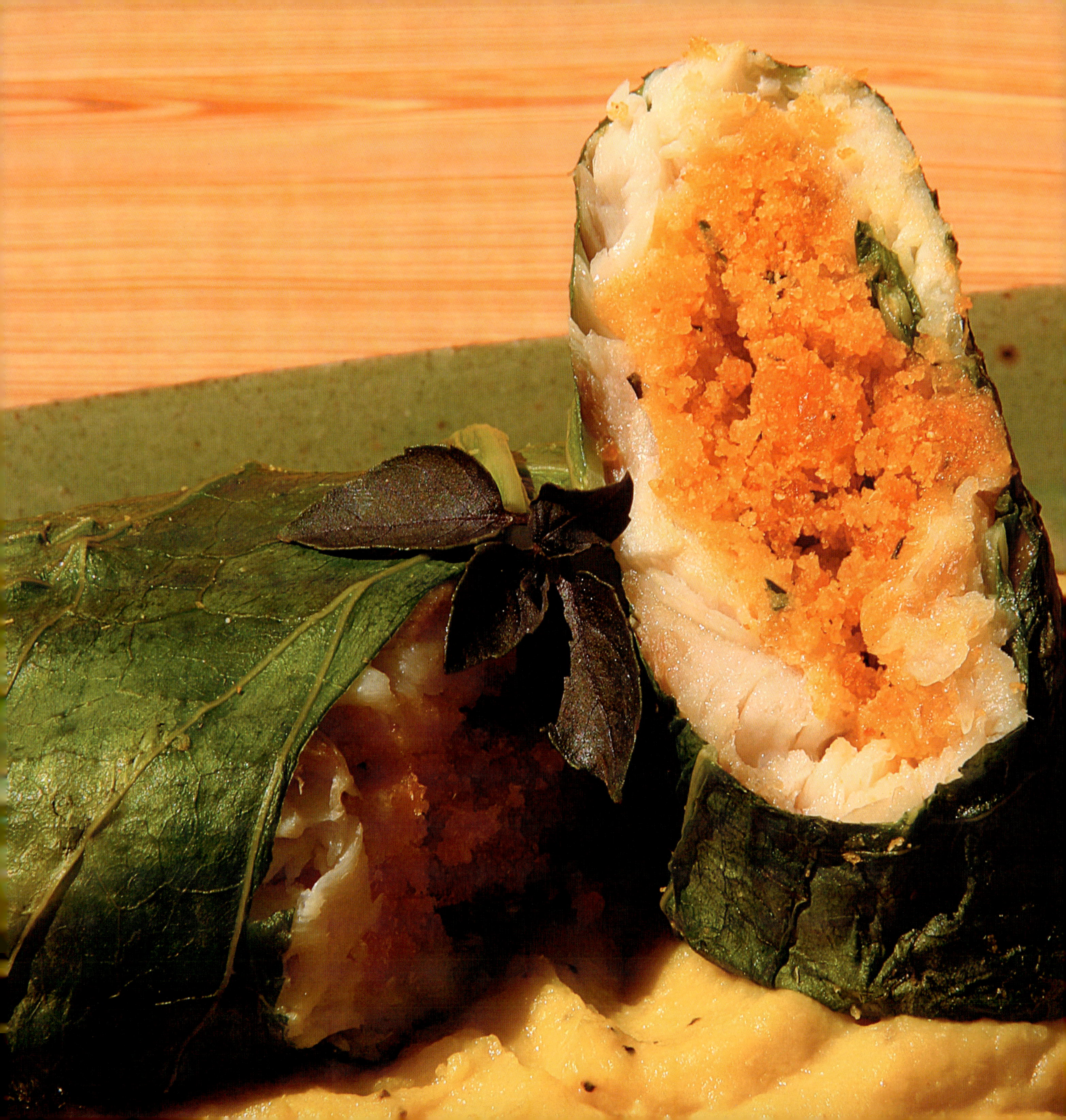

Stuffed sea bass with shrimp farofa
wrapped in kale with plantain purée

600 g sea bass fillets
juice of 1 lemon
salt and pepper to taste
4 kale leaves, pre-cooked, to assemble
aluminum foil

♪ Preparation: season fillets with salt, lemon and pepper, and set aside.

♪ Shrimp *farofa*: 100 *ml* olive oil / 10 g garlic, smashed / 200 g onions / 300 g prawns, peeled / 100 *ml* tomato sauce / parsley to taste / 300 g cassava flour / salt and pepper to taste

♪ Preparation: heat olive oil in a skillet, and fry garlic and onion; add shrimp and cook for a few minutes. Add tomato sauce, parsley and cassava flour little by little. Season with salt and pepper.

♪ Plantain purée: 4 overripe plantains / 200 *ml* milk / 120 *ml* coconut milk / 1 coffee spoon ginger / 4 tablespoons honey / 120 *ml* heavy cream / salt and pepper to taste

♪ Preparation: cook plantains until tender. Blend milk, coconut milk, ginger and honey. Return to heat and pour heavy cream. Cook for a few minutes. Season with salt and pepper.

♪ To assemble: cut kale leaves in halves and top them with sea bass fillet. Top it with *farofa* and roll each portion with the kale leaf as a roll cake. Sprinkle olive oil and wrap them up in aluminum foil. Place in oven for about 15 minutes. To serve, place plantain purée in the center of the plate; slice fish rolls and place them on top of purée.

♪ Servings: 4 portions

♪ Preparation time: 1 hour and 30 minutes

Grilled flounder
with pinyon and green salad

4 flounder fillets (800 g)
juice of 1 lemon
salt and pepper to taste
olive oil to grill

♪ Preparation: season flounder fillets with salt, lemon and pepper. Grill them in olive oil.

♪ Sautéed *pinyon*: 200 g pinyons / 60 g unsalted butter / parsley to taste / salt to taste

♪ Preparation: cook pinyons in a pressure cooker with water and salt for about 30 minutes. Peel and sauté them in butter. Sprinkle parsley and salt.

♪ Green salad: green-leaf lettuce / Boston lettuce / rocket / watercress

♪ Preparation: wash leaves very well and season them with a lemon and olive oil dressing.

♪ To assemble: place salad on half of plate and fish on the other half, topped with pinyons.

♪ Servings: 4 portions

♪ Preparation time: 1 hour

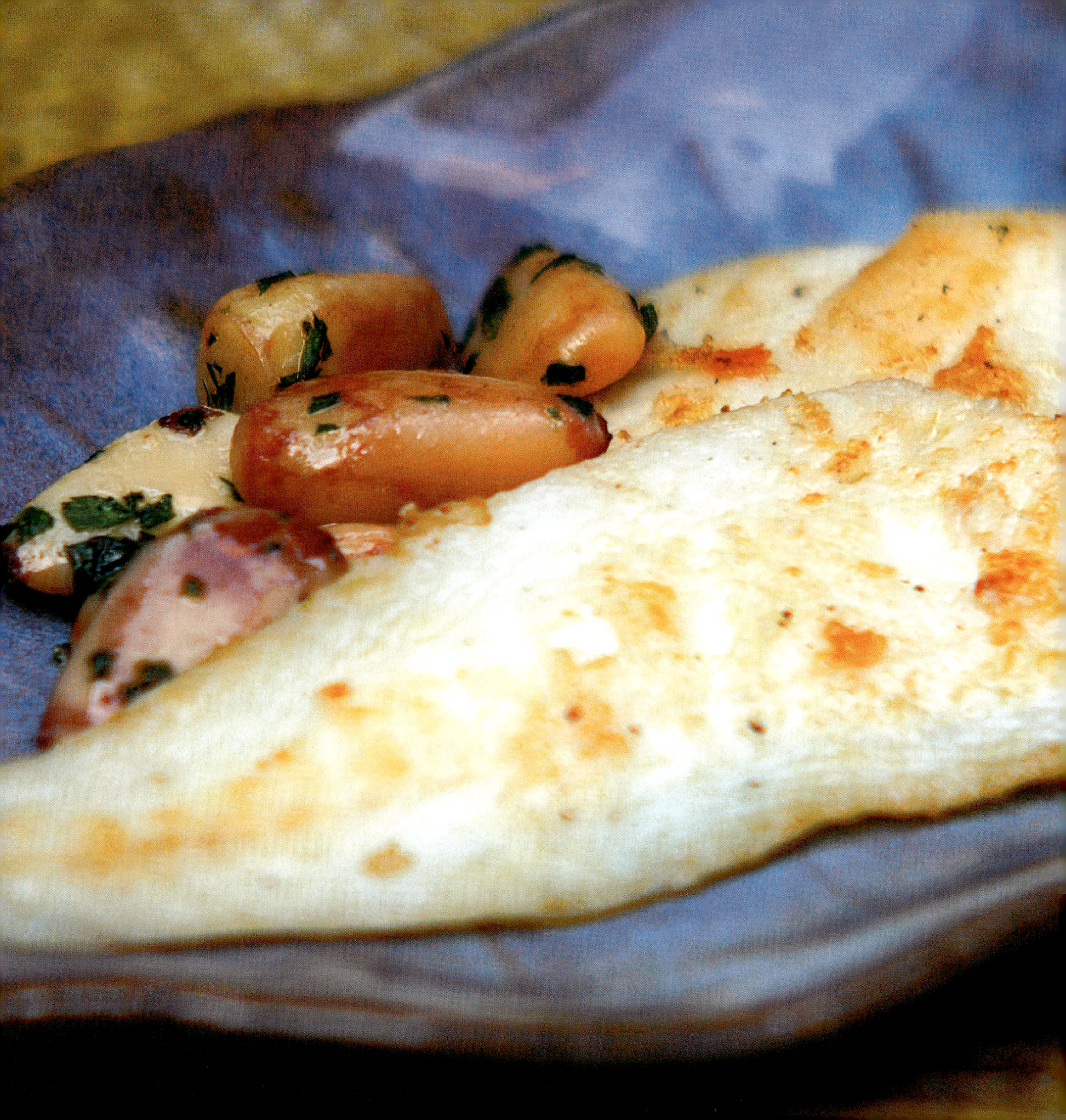

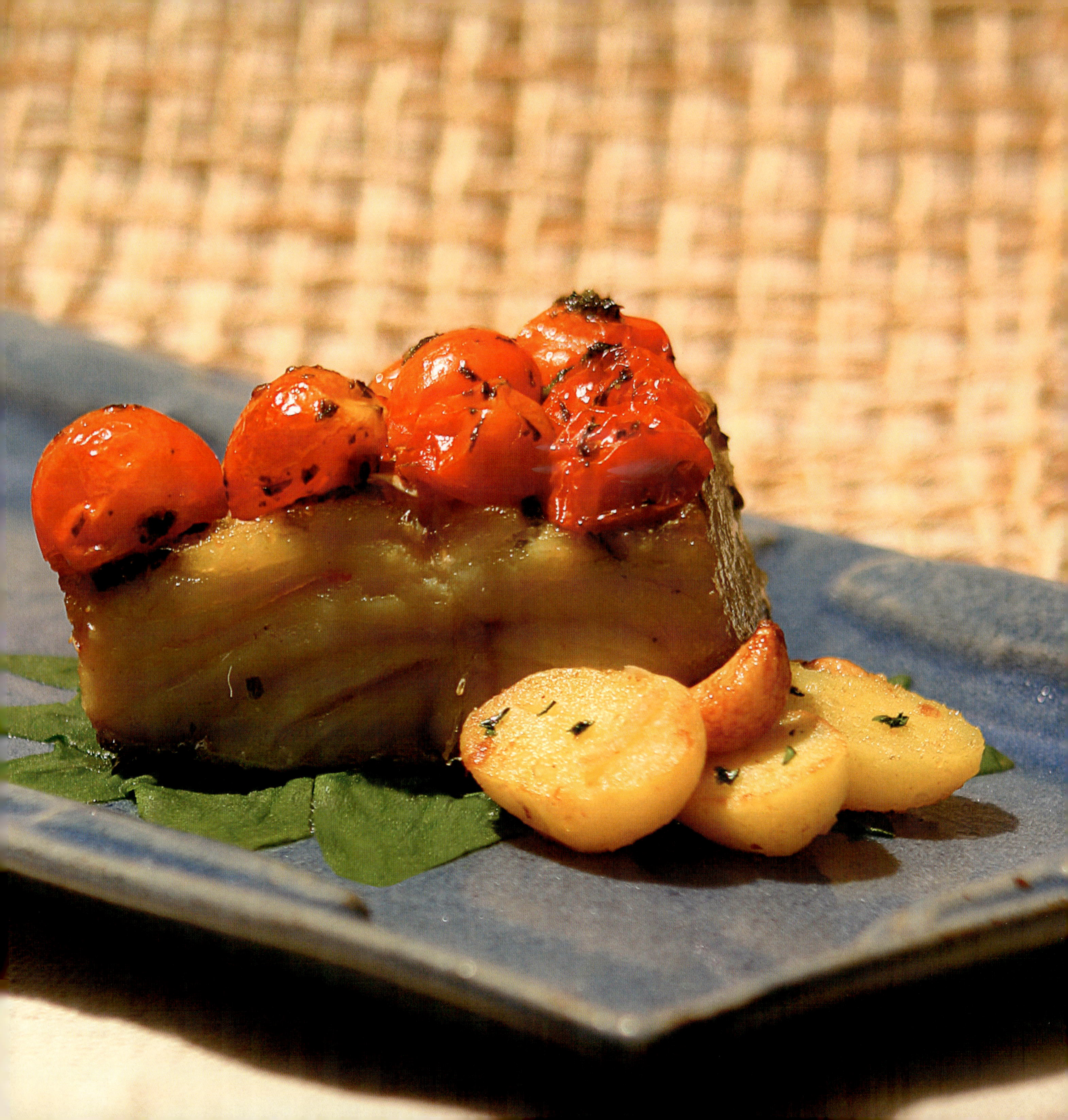

Roasted cod chunks with tomato *confit*,
sautéed spinach and golden potatoes

♪ Roasted cod:
1 kg cod loin, previously desalted
1 *l* milk
24 pear tomatoes

♪ Parsley pesto:
600 *ml* olive oil
juice of 1 lemon
200 g parsley
salt and pepper to taste

♪ Preparation: cook cod in milk for about 20 minutes. Meanwhile, blend all pesto ingredients. Place cod in baking sheet, spread part of parsley pesto and cover it with pear tomato halves. Roast for about 15 minutes.

♪ Spinach sauté: 60 g garlic, smashed / 100 *ml* olive oil / 800 g spinach leaves / salt and pepper to taste

♪ Preparation: fry garlic in olive oil until golden brown. Add spinach leaves and let them wilt. Season with salt and pepper and set aside.

♪ Golden potatoes: 300 g baby potatoes / 100 *ml* olive oil / parsley to taste / salt to taste

♪ Preparation: cook potatoes with skin until tender. Peel and cut them in halves. Heat olive oil in a skillet and sauté potatoes until brown. Add parsley and salt.

♪ To assemble: on a plate, toss spinach leaves and top them with cod fillet. Circle salad and cod with golden potatoes and top fish with the remaining pesto.

♪ Servings: 4 portions

♪ Preparation time: 1 hour

Snook with cashew nut crust, *vatapá* and sautéed yellow yam

(*Vatapá* is a typical Brazilian dish made of dende oil (palm oil), coconut milk, ginger, peanuts and is usually served with shrimp or fish and white rice)

800 g snook (thick fillet)
juice of 1 lemon
salt and pepper to taste
olive oil to grill

♪ Cashew nut crust: 200 g cashew nuts, processed into a coarse meal / 150 g unsalted butter / 200 g breadcrumbs (made of homemade toasts, preferably) / salt and pepper to taste

♪ Preparation: season snook with lemon, salt, pepper and olive oil and set aside. Mix all cashew nut crust ingredients until you obtain a coarse meal. Place this *farofa* on top of seasoned fish in a baking sheet and place it in oven at 180°C for 25 minutes.

♪ Vatapá: 50 g stale French bread loaves, sliced / 1 *l* milk / 2 tablespoons dende oil (palm oil) / 10 g garlic cloves, smashed / 200 g onions, chopped / 50 g red bell peppers, chopped / 50 g yellow bell peppers, chopped / 200 g fresh shrimps, peeled / 200 *ml* coconut milk / 30 g tomatoes, chopped / 20 g peanuts / 30 g cashew nuts / 10 g ginger, grated / salt and pepper to taste

♪ Preparation: in a bowl, soak bread in milk for 15 minutes. Heat dende oil in a skillet, fry garlic until golden brown and add onion, bell peppers and shrimps and cook for a few minutes. Add coconut milk, chopped tomatoes, peanuts, cashew nuts and ginger. Season with salt and pepper. Blend everything with soaked bread. Do it little by little, pausing, since the ingredients will form a heavy batter, difficult to blend (if necessary, add some water). Place the mixture in a saucepan and stir very well. Cook for some minutes more, stirring constantly not to boil.

♪ Yellow yam *sautée*: 400 g yellow yam / water to cook / 2 tablespoons butter / salt and pepper to taste / parsley to taste

♪ Preparation: slice yellow yam. Cook in water with salt until *al dente*. In a skillet, melt butter to sauté yam. Add parsley, salt and pepper.

♪ To assemble: on a plate, place *vatapá* in the center, top it with snook and surround it with yam.

♪ Servings: 4 portions

♪ Preparation time: 1 hour and 30 minutes

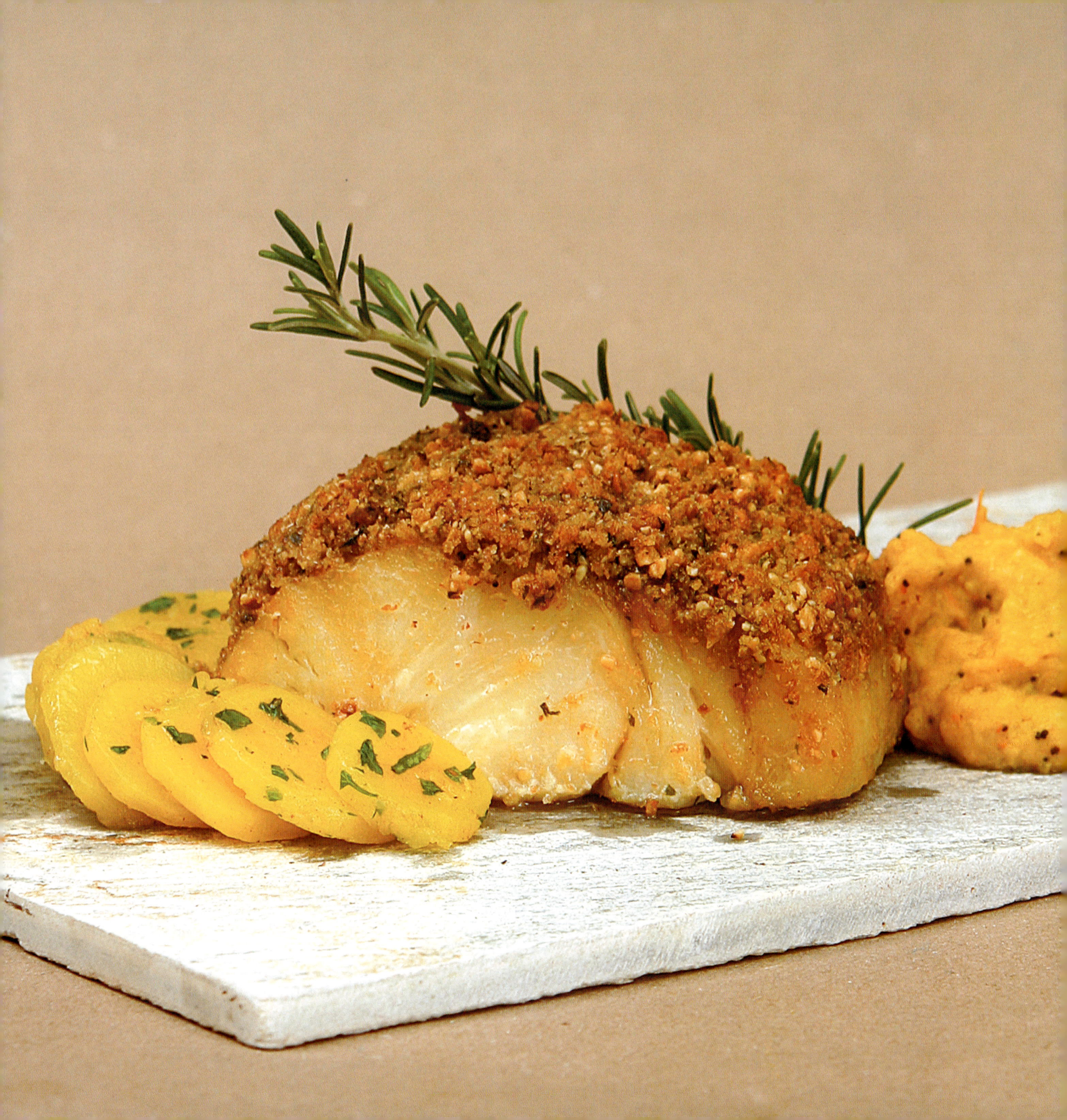

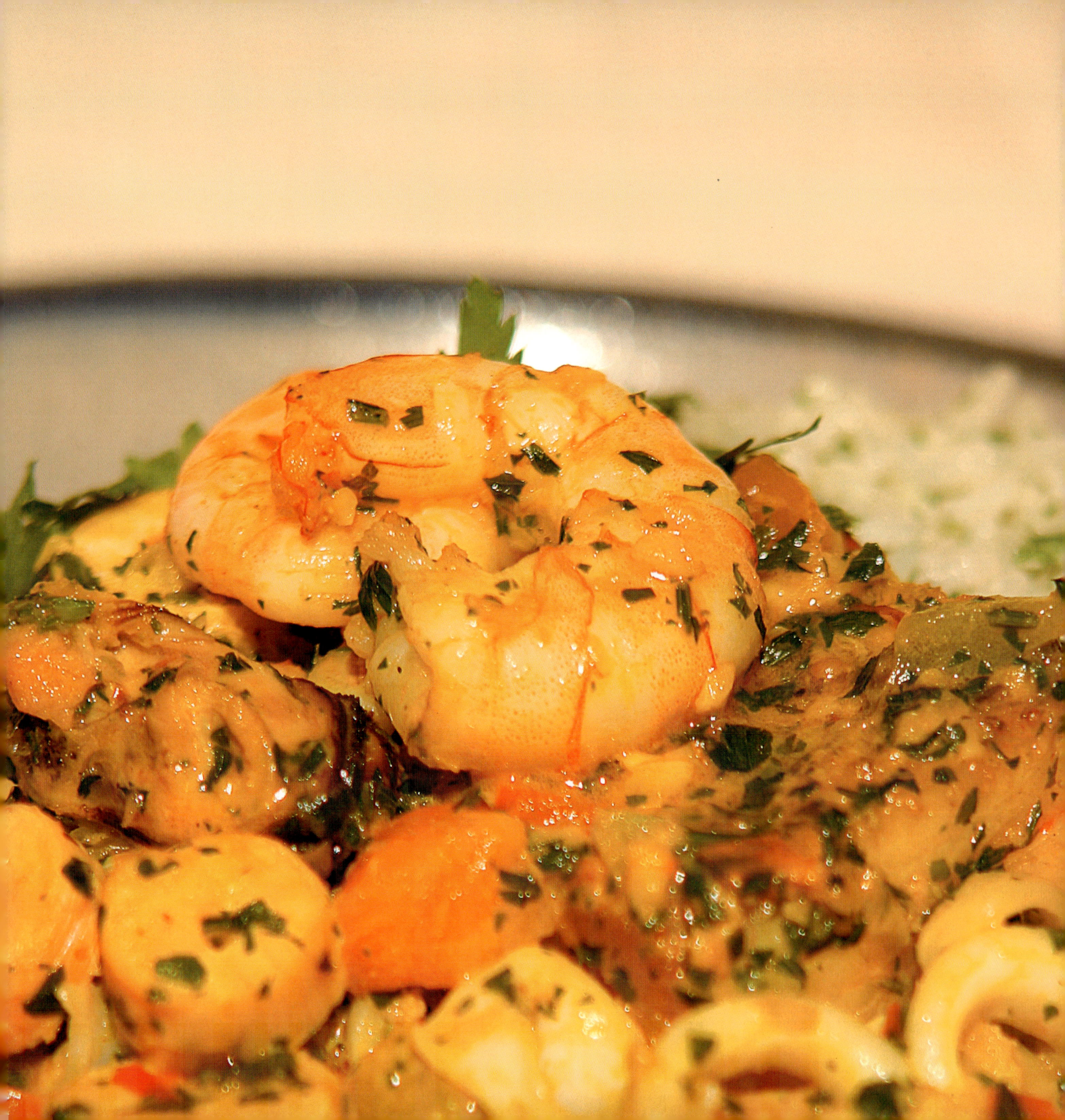

Seafood *Moqueca*
with coconut rice
(Moqueca is a traditional Brazilian stew, prepared with fish and/or seafood, dende oil (palm oil) and coconut milk)

200 g sea bass fillet
2 tablespoons dende oil (palm oil)
4 garlic cloves, smashed
250 g onions
120 g red bell peppers
120 g yellow bell peppers
200 g tomatoes
200 g squid rings
200 g medium shrimps, clean
120 g octopuses, diced
120 g vongoli, clean
200 ml coconut milk
juice of 1 lemon
salt and red pepper to taste
parsley to taste

♪ Preparation: season sea bass fillets with lemon, salt and pepper and set aside. Heat dende oil in a skillet and fry garlic and onion. Add diced bell peppers and cook for a few minutes. Add tomatoes and seafood: squids, shrimps, octopuses and vongoli. Sauté for a few minutes. Add coconut milk, and finally, the sea bass fillet. Cook for about 15 minutes or until fish is cooked. Add parsley.

♪ Coconut rice: 300 g white rice, cooked / 150 ml coconut milk / 100 g coconut, grated / salt to taste / parsley to taste

♪ Preparation: in a saucepan, mix coconut milk and grated coconut to cooked rice. Taste to adjust salt. Sprinkle chopped parsley.

♪ To assemble: on a serving dish or individual plates, place *moqueca* beside coconut rice.

♪ Servings: 4 portions

♪ Preparation time: 1 hour

Snook medallion with smoked catfish, pumpkin purée, fried kale and cherry pepper

8 snook medallion (1 kg)
160 g smoked catfish carpaccio
100 ml olive oil
juice of 1 lemon
salt and pepper to taste

♪ Preparation: season medallions with lemon, salt and pepper. Heat olive oil in a skillet, and grill medallions. Slice smoked catfish thinly into 8 slices. Place one medallion on top of each slice and roll it.

♪ Pumpkin purée: 800 g pumpkin / water to cook / 200 ml milk / 100 g butter / salt and pepper to taste

♪ Preparation: cook pumpkin in water with salt. When tender, blend it slowing pouring milk into blender. Return to heat, add butter and season with salt and pepper.

♪ Fried kale: 200 g kale / oil to fry / salt to taste / 1 cherry pepper to garnish

♪ Preparation: thinly slice kale leaves and fry them in hot oil with salt.

♪ To assemble: place medallions in the center, top them with fried kale and garnish with pumpkin purée and slices of cherry pepper.

♪ Servings: 4 portions

♪ Preparation time: 1 hour

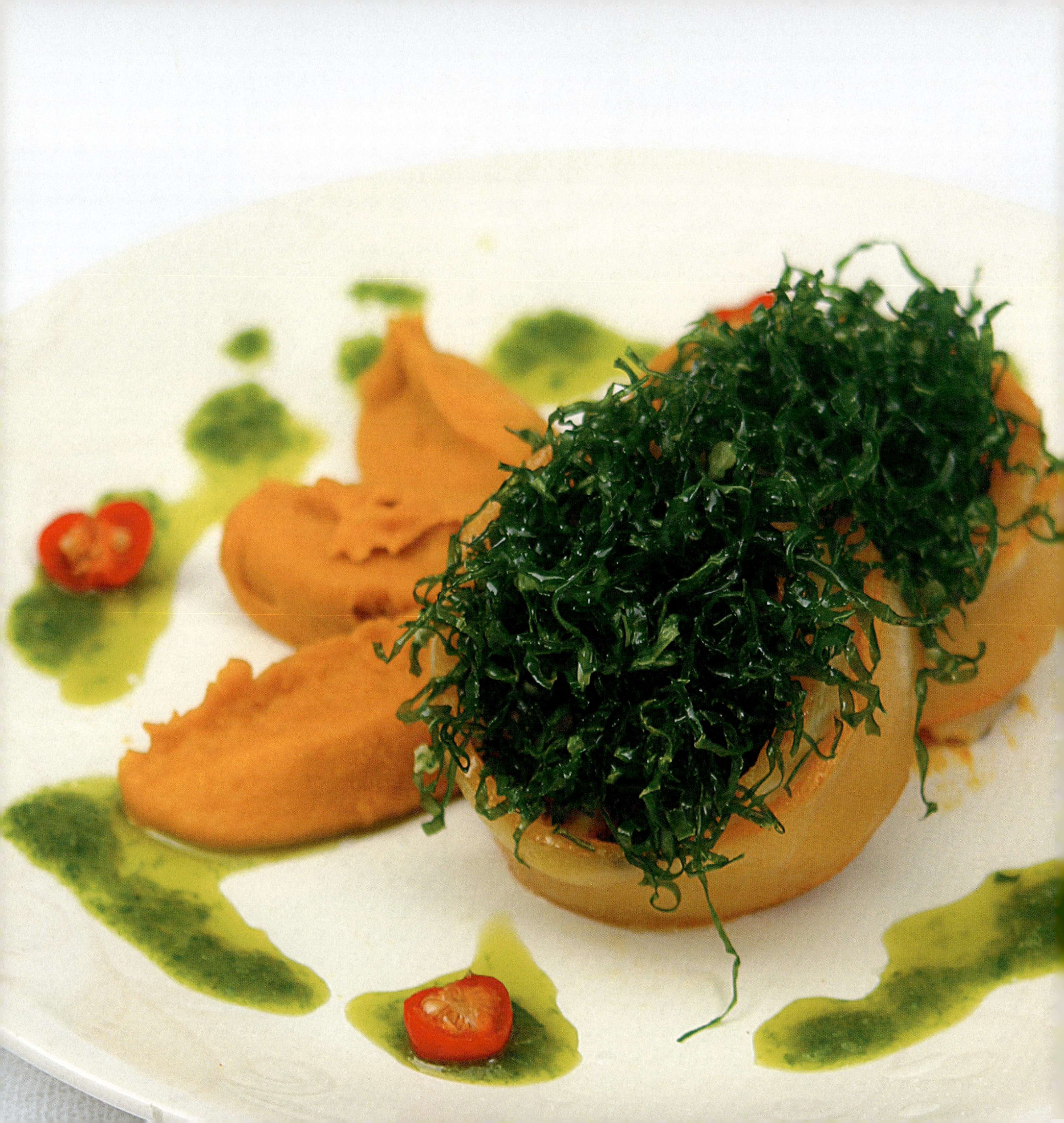

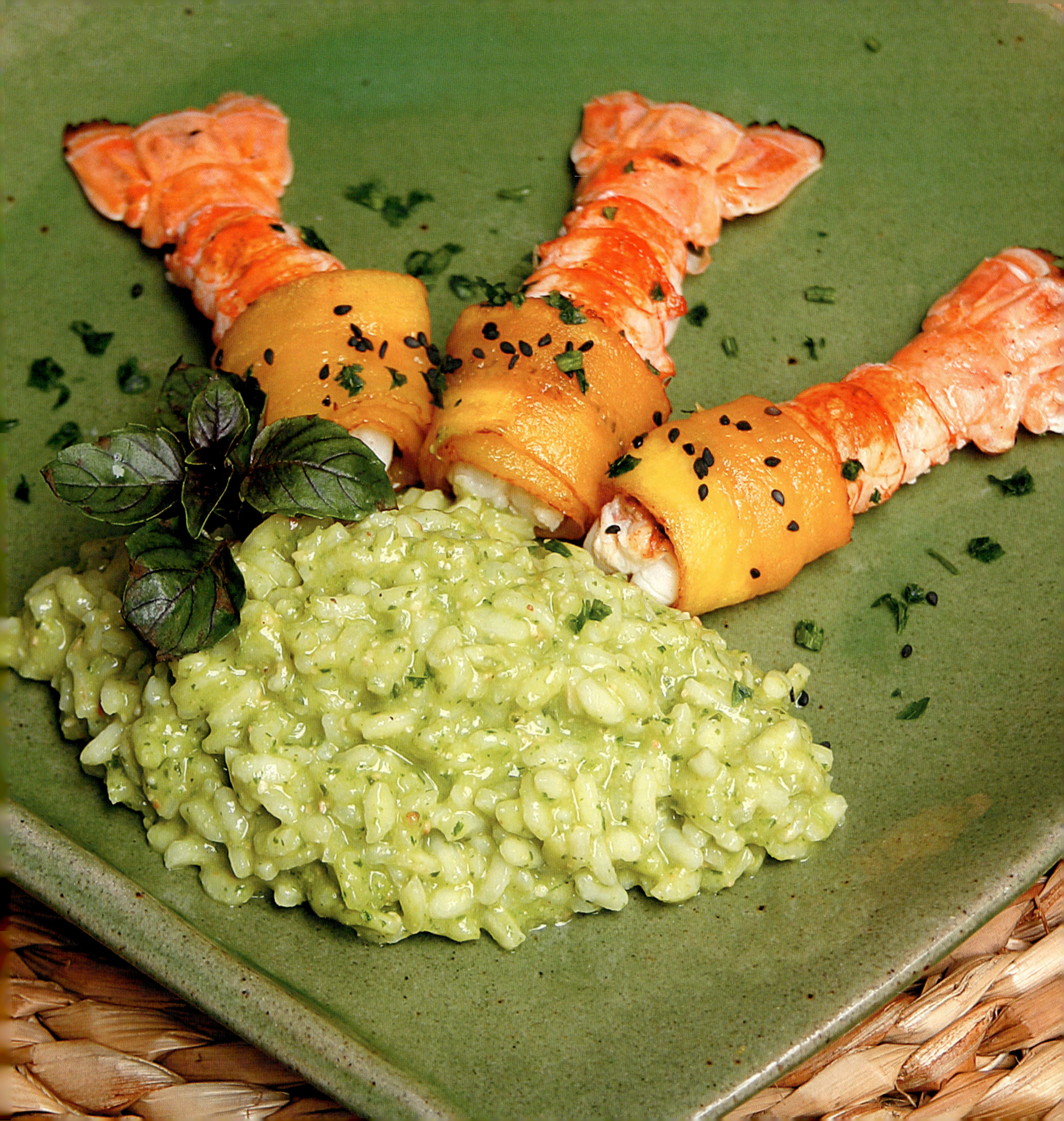

Grilled langoustines with plantains
and herb risotto

12 large langoustines
2 overripe plantains
100 ml olive oil
juice of 1 lemon
salt and pepper to taste

♪ Preparation: season langoustines with salt, pepper and lemon. Heat olive oil in a skillet and grill langoustines. Set aside. Thinly slice plantain lengthwise and grill in olive oil. Wrap grilled langoustines with plantain.

♪ Herb risotto: 2 l vegetable broth / 250 g onions, chopped / 60 g butter / 240 g arborio rice / 200 ml white wine / 50 g fresh herbs (basil and parsley), chopped.

♪ Preparation: sauté onion in 1 tablespoon butter. Add rice and cook for about 2 minutes, stirring constantly. Add wine and stir until it evaporates. Add one cup of vegetable broth (which must be very hot) and stir well. Repeat procedure until all broth has been absorbed, for about 20 minutes. Finally, add fresh herbs and the remaining butter. Season with salt and pepper.

♪ To assemble: serve langoustines side by side with risotto garnished with stig of basil.

♪ Servings: 4 portions

♪ Preparation time: 1 hour and 30 minutes

Crab frittata

600 g crab meat
30 g garlic, smashed
300 g onions, chopped
100 ml olive oil
100 g red bell peppers, diced
50 g green bell peppers, diced
50 g yellow bell peppers, diced
500 ml coconut milk
3 eggs
salt and pepper
parsley or cilantro to taste

♪ Preparation: fry garlic, salt, pepper and onion in olive oil. If prefered, use parsley or cilantro. Add bell peppers and sauté for a few minutes. Add crab meat and cook for some minutes more. Add coconut milk and cook for about 5 minutes. Whisk egg whites until they form stiff peaks. Add egg yolks and continue beating until all ingredients are well mixed. Pour half of the beaten eggs into sautéed crab and mix well. Top this mixture with the remaining beaten eggs, without mixing. Place it in oven for about 30 minutes, or until brown.

♪ Servings: 4 portions

♪ Preparation time: 1 hour and 30 minutes

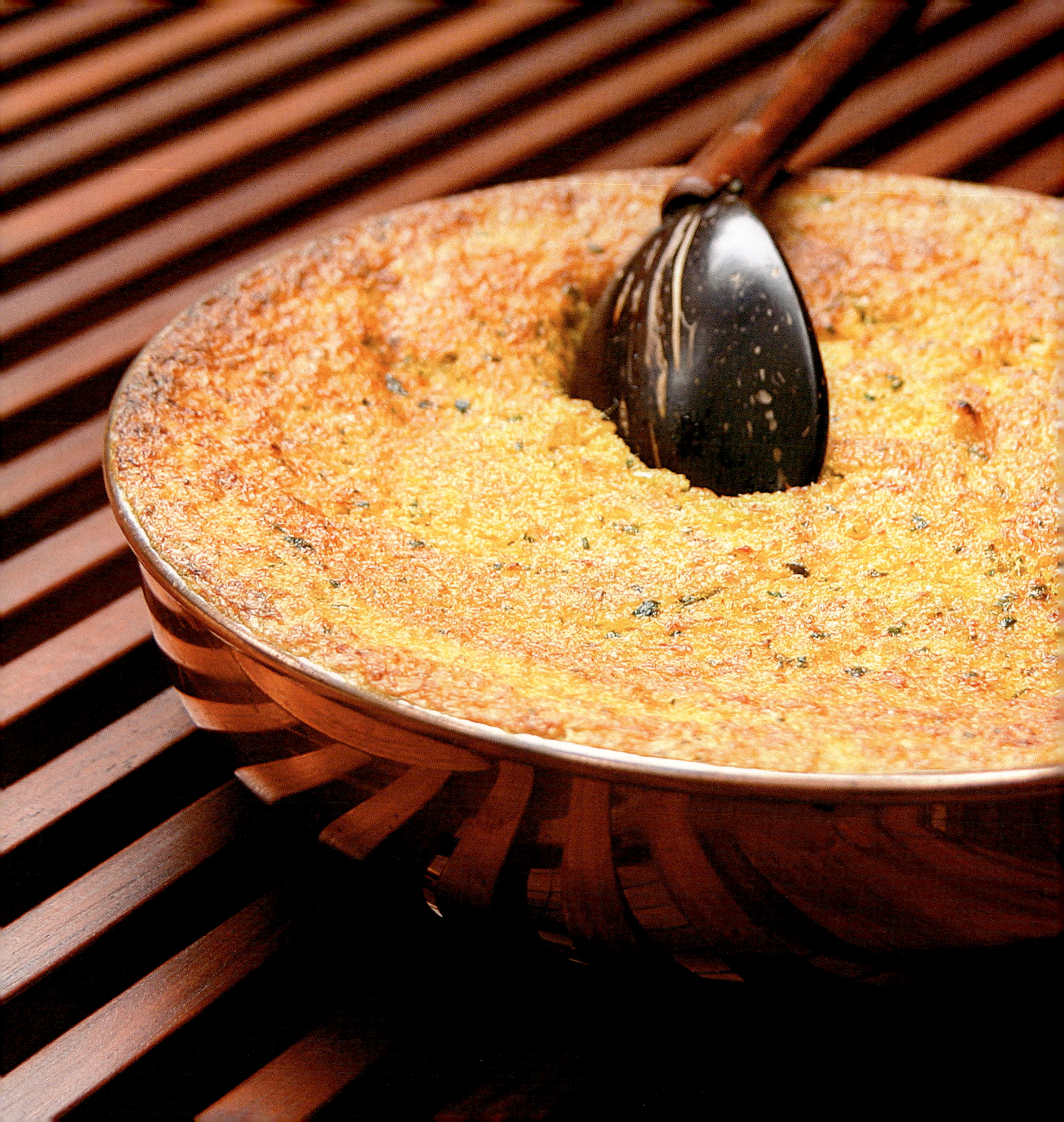

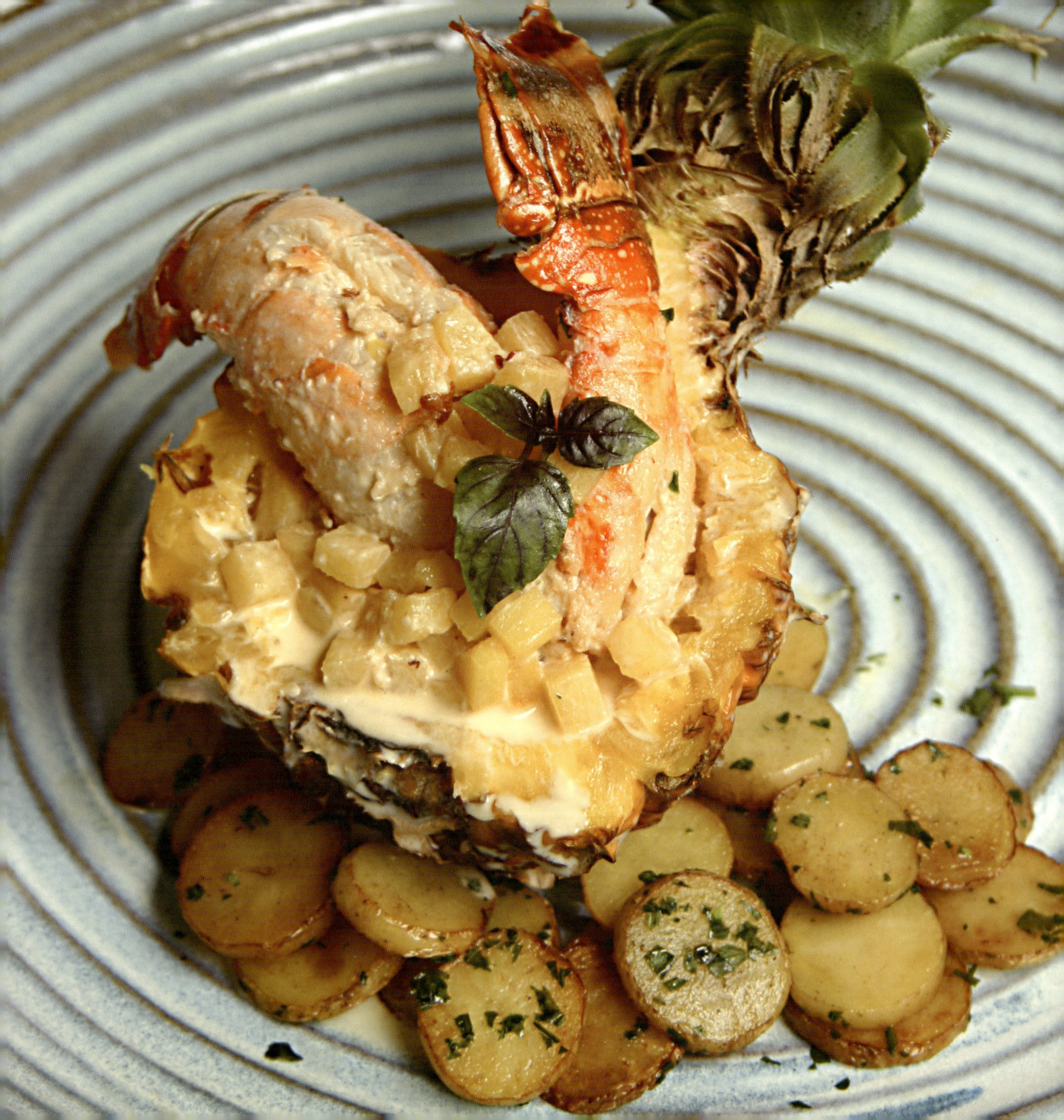

Lobster grilled in pineapple
with sautéed potatoes

12 medium lobster tails
juice of 2 lemons
salt and pepper to taste
2 pineapples
60 g butter
30 g garlic
olive oil
150 g onions
60 ml vodka
400 ml cream
basil to taste

♪ Preparation: season lobster with lemon, salt and pepper and set aside. Cut pineapple in half and remove center. Dice half pineapple, blend the other half and set aside. In a skillet, brown garlic in olive oil, add onion and sauté. Add lobsters and grill slightly. Add vodka and flambé. Then, add cream. Taste to adjust seasoning, and add basil leaves. Place it into pineapple shell, sprinkle grated Parmesan cheese and place it in the oven for 3 minutes, to brown.

♪ Sautéed potato: 600 g baby potatoes / 1 tablespoon butter / salt and parsley to taste

♪ Preparation: cook potatoes with skin until tender. Peel and cut them in halves. Melt butter in a skillet and add potatoes. Season with salt and add parsley.

♪ To assemble: on a plate, place the lobster grilled in pineapple in the center and garnish with potatoes.

♪ Servings: 4 portions

♪ Preparation time: 1 hour

Shrimp stew with curry and coconut milk
with steamed vegetables

1 kg large shrimps with tail, peeled
juice of 1 lemon
salt and pepper to taste

♪ Preparation: season shrimps with lemon, salt and pepper and set aside.

♪ Steamed vegetables: 100 g broccolis / 100 g carrots, sliced / 100 g chayotes, sliced / 100 g fresh peas / 100 g green beans / 100 g zucchinis / salt to taste

♪ Preparation: steam vegetables, separately, until *al dente* and set aside.

♪ Sauce: 30 g butter / 5 garlic cloves, smashed / 1 onion, chopped / 1 pinch curry / 3 lemongrass roots / 400 *ml* coconut milk / salt and pepper to taste / parsley to taste

♪ Preparation: in a skillet, fry garlic and onion in butter. Add curry, mixing to dissolve it. Add shrimp and lemongrass root and sauté for some minutes more. Pour coconut milk. Cook for a few minutes.

♪ To assemble: harmoniously place shrimps and steamed vegetables on plates, and serve.

♪ Servings: 4 portions

♪ Preparation time: 45 minutes

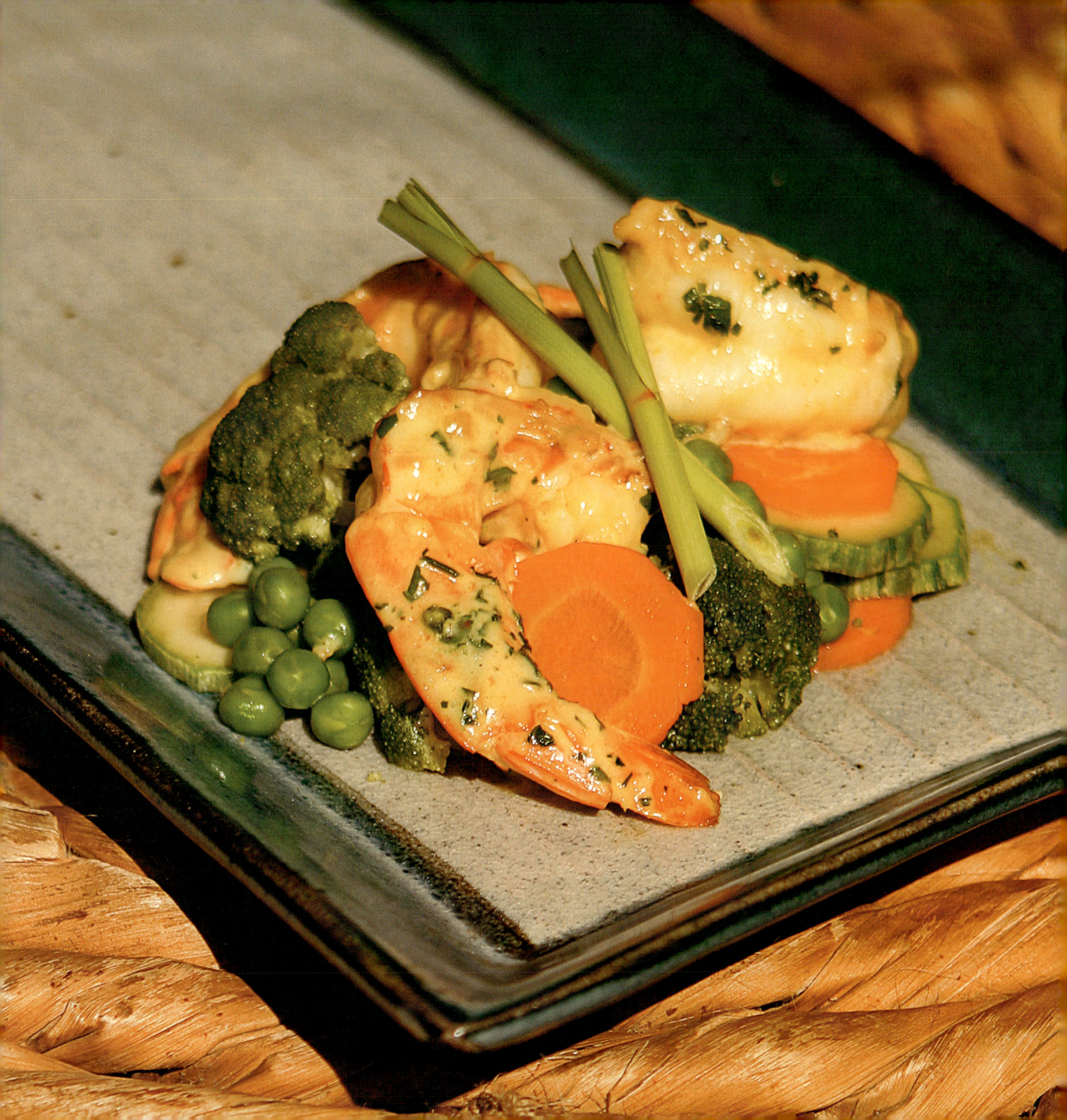

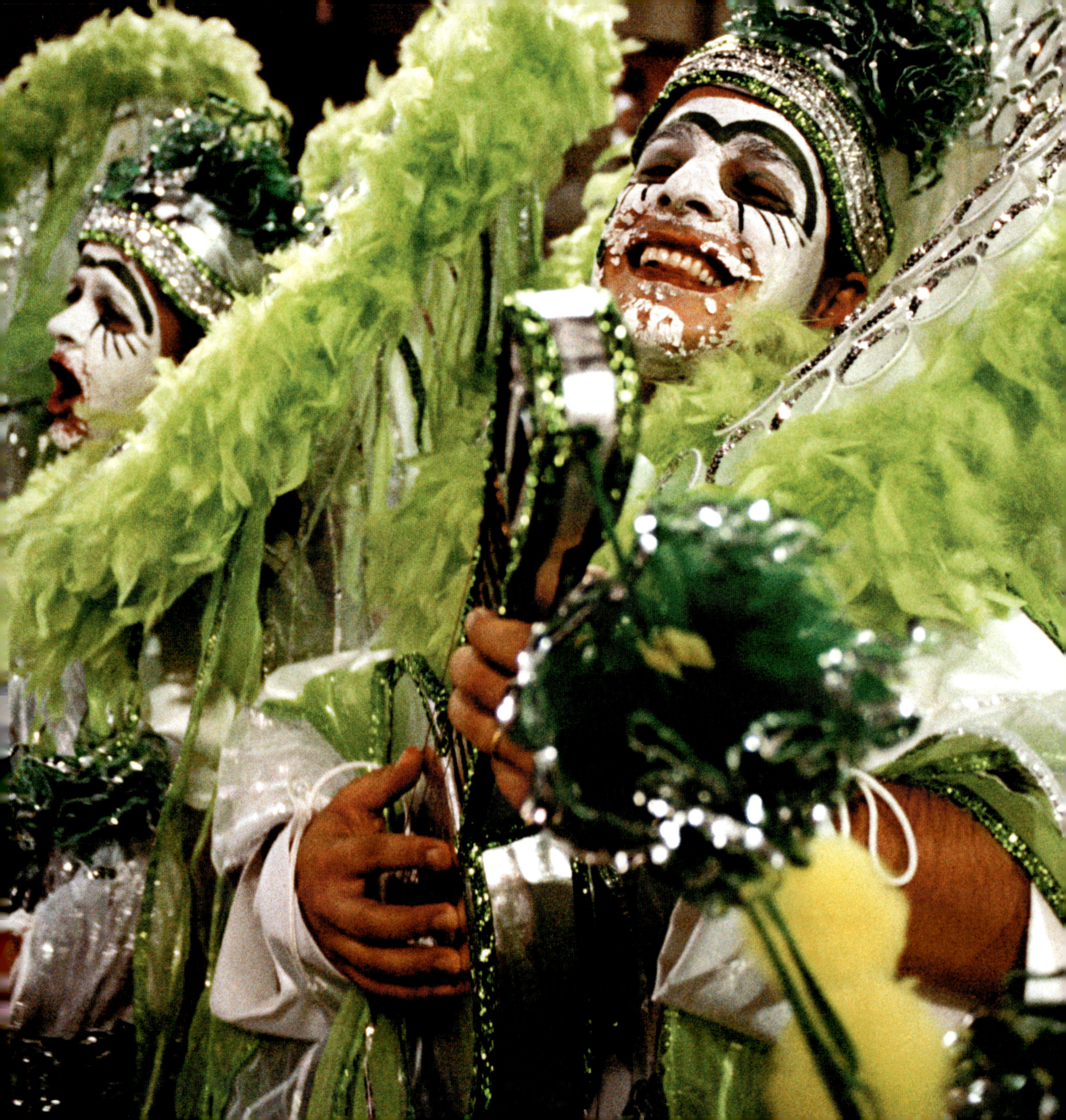

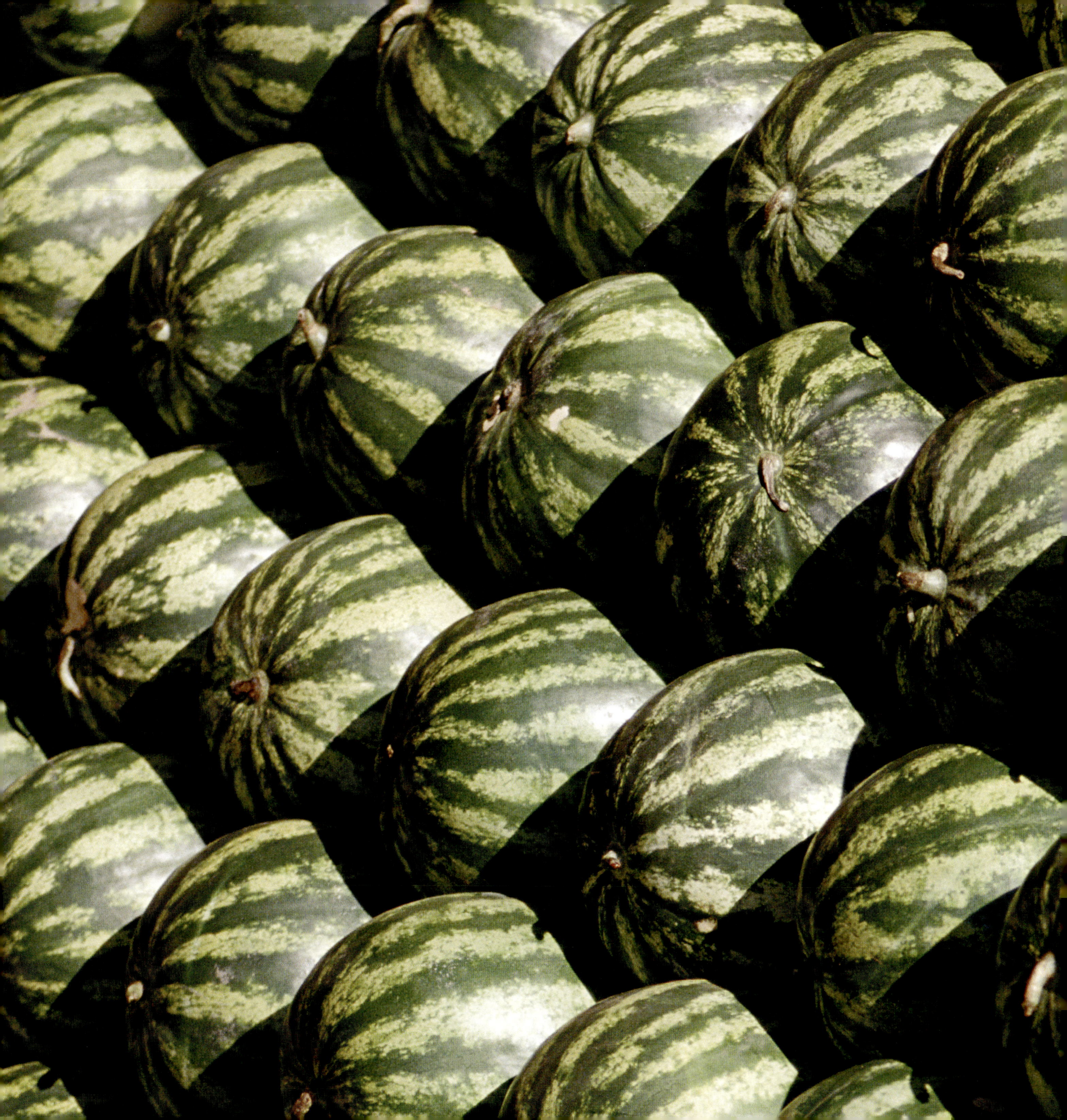

"Para viver um grande amor

[...]

Conta ponto saber fazer coisinhas

Ovos mexidos, camarões, sopinhas

Molhos, filés com fritas, comidinhas

Para depois do amor

E o que há de melhor que ir pra cozinha

E preparar com amor uma galinha

Com uma rica e gostosa farofinha

Para o seu grande amor?"

♪ Vinicius de Moraes & Toquinho, Para viver um grande amor

Brazil nut pudding : p. 114

Lemongrass crème brulée : p. 116

Tapioca pudding : p. 118

Crystallized banana pie : p. 120

Cupuaçu pie : p. 122

Squash and coconut terrine : p. 124

Pineapple with mint in a almond web : p. 126

Starfruit flambéed : p. 128

DESSERTS

Brazil nut pudding

♪ **Pudding:**
1 can condensed milk
350 ml milk
3 eggs

♪ **Preparation:** blender condensed milk, milk and eggs, until all ingredients mix well. Set aside.

♪ **Batter:**
60 g unsalted butter
200 g sugar
100 ml milk
200 g all-purpose flour
200 g Brazil nuts, crushed

♪ **Preparation:** cream butter and sugar, add flour, Brazil nuts and milk. Set aside.

♪ **Caramel:** 500 g sugar / 1 l water

♪ **Preparation:** mix sugar and water in a saucepan until sugar dissolves. Heat it for about 10 minutes without stirring until brown. Pour caramel into ramekins. Top it with Brazil nut cream and finally with the condensed milk mixture. Bake at 180°C in bain marie for about 25 minutes.

♪ **Servings:** 10 portions

♪ **Preparation time:** 1 hour and 30 minutes

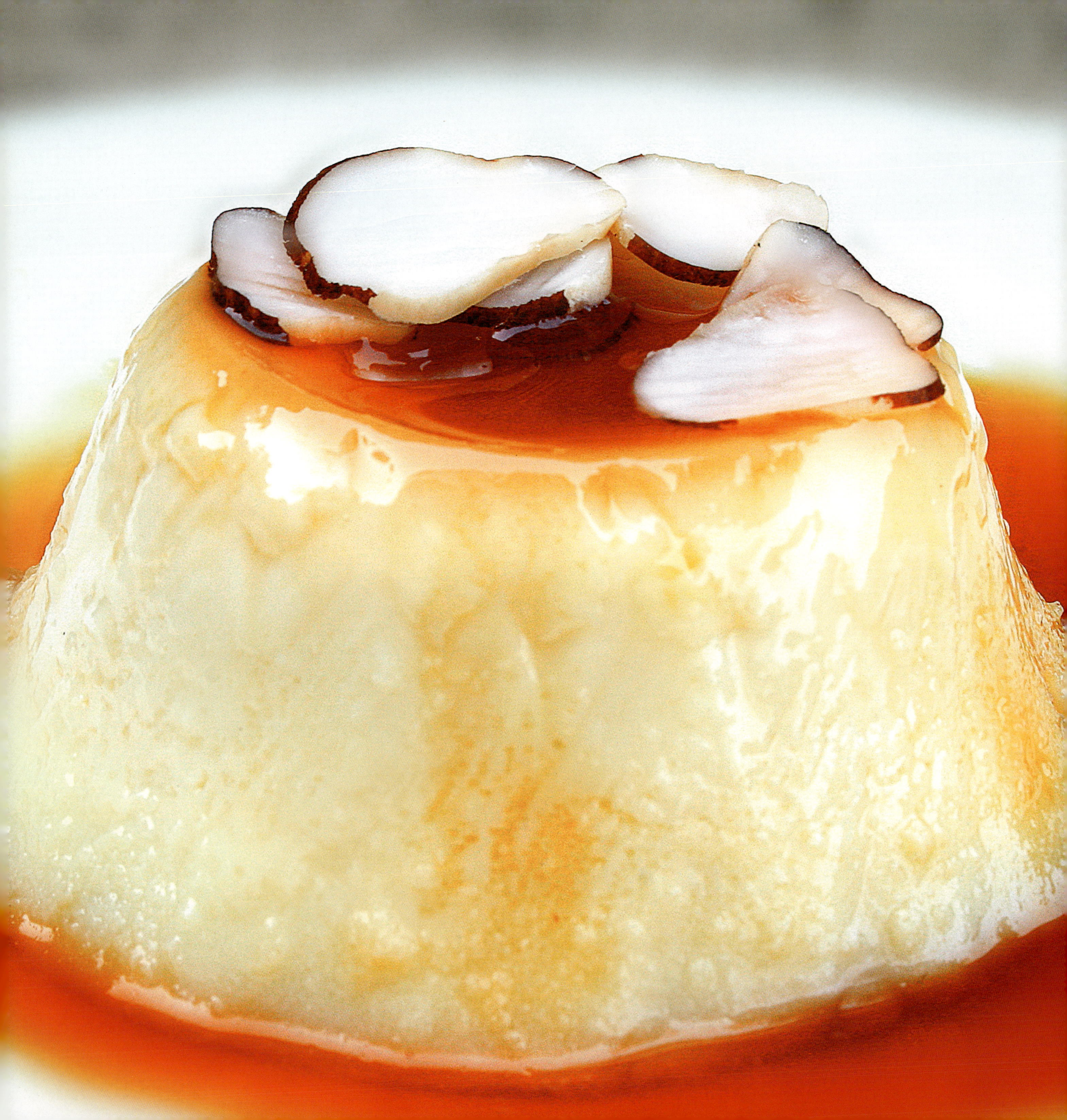

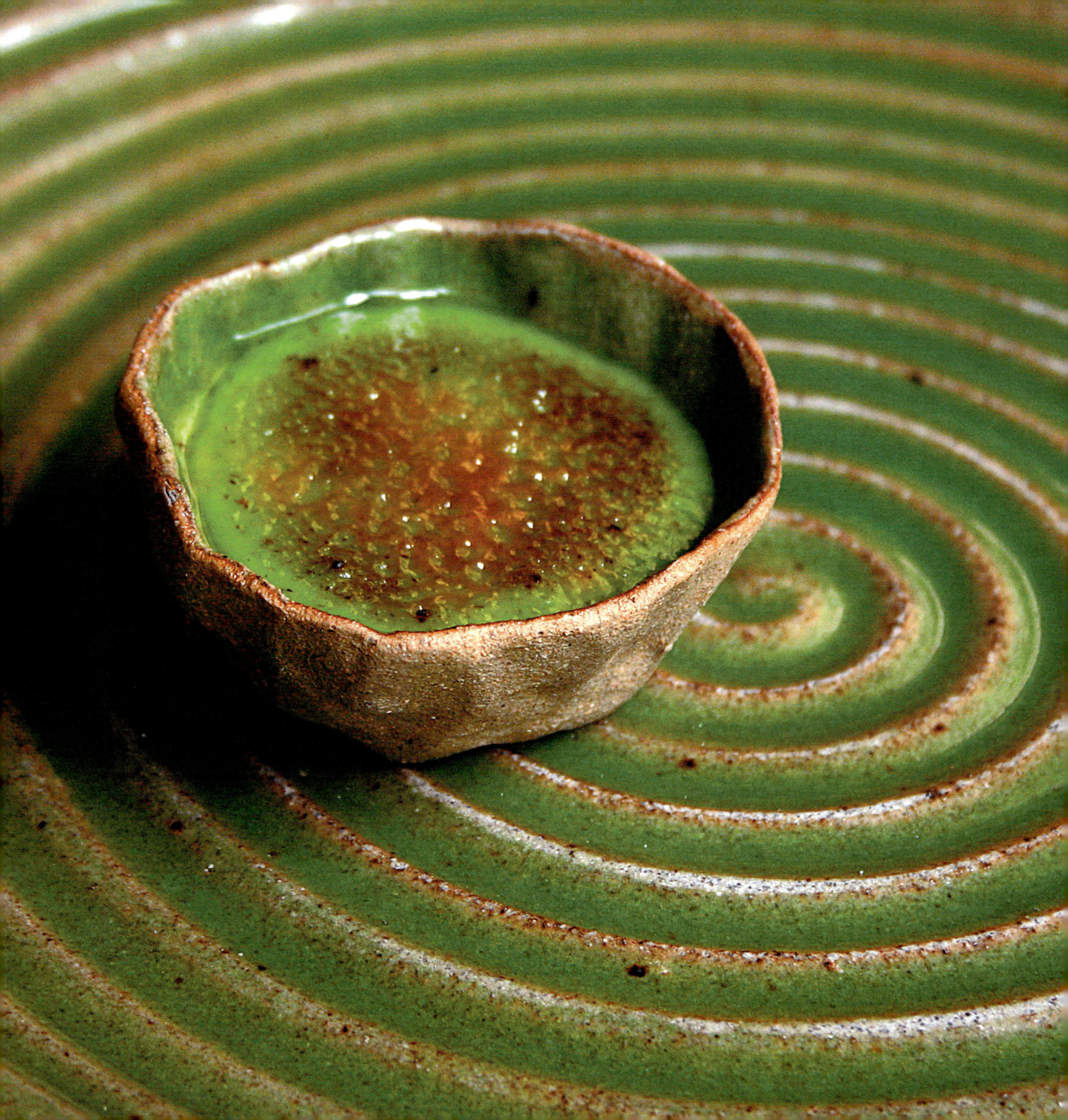

Lemongrass crème brulée

500 g lemongrass leaves
100 ml milk
1 1/2 l cream
10 egg yolks
120 g sugar
100 g brown sugar

♪ Preparation: blend lemongrass with milk and strain. Add heavy cream and cook. Beat egg yolks with sugar, until thick and light yellow. When lemongrass cream is cool, add egg yolk mixture. Distribute into ramekins and cover with aluminum foil. Bake at 180°C in bain marie for about 15 minutes. Remove from heat, leave it to cool and refrigerate until firm. Just prior to serving, sprinkle brown sugar and caramelize it with a blowtorch.

♪ Servings: 12 portions

♪ Preparation time: 45 minutes

Tapioca pudding

500 *ml* coconut milk
500 *ml* milk
250 g tapioca
50 g coconut, grated
5 eggs
1 can condensed milk
1 can cream

♪ Caramelo: 500 g sugar / 1 *l* water

♪ Preparation: combine milk, coconut milk, tapioca and grated coconut in a bowl. Let it rest for about 30 minutes, or until tapioca absorbs all liquid. Prepare caramel: place sugar and water in a saucepan and stir until sugar dissolves. Heat for about 10 minutes without stirring. When brown, remove from heat. Spread caramel in a bundt pan using the back of a spoon. Blend eggs, cream and condensed milk. Add to tapioca mixture. Pour into caramelized bundt pan and cover it with aluminum foil. Bake in bain marie for about 1 hour. Open the oven, take foil away and insert a stick into it. If it comes out clean, the pudding is ready. Chill, remove from pan and refrigerate.

♪ Servings: 10 portions

♪ Preparation time: 2 hours

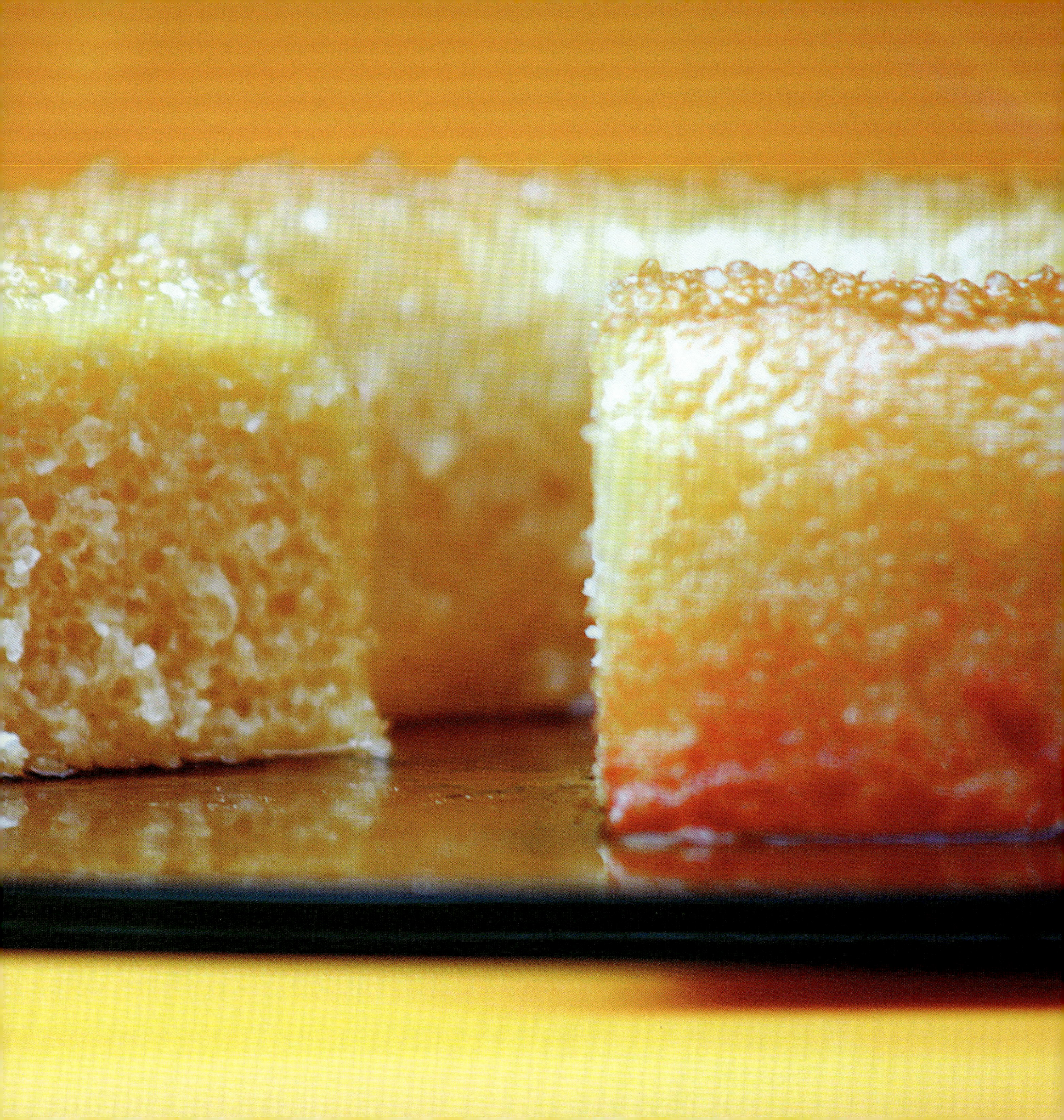

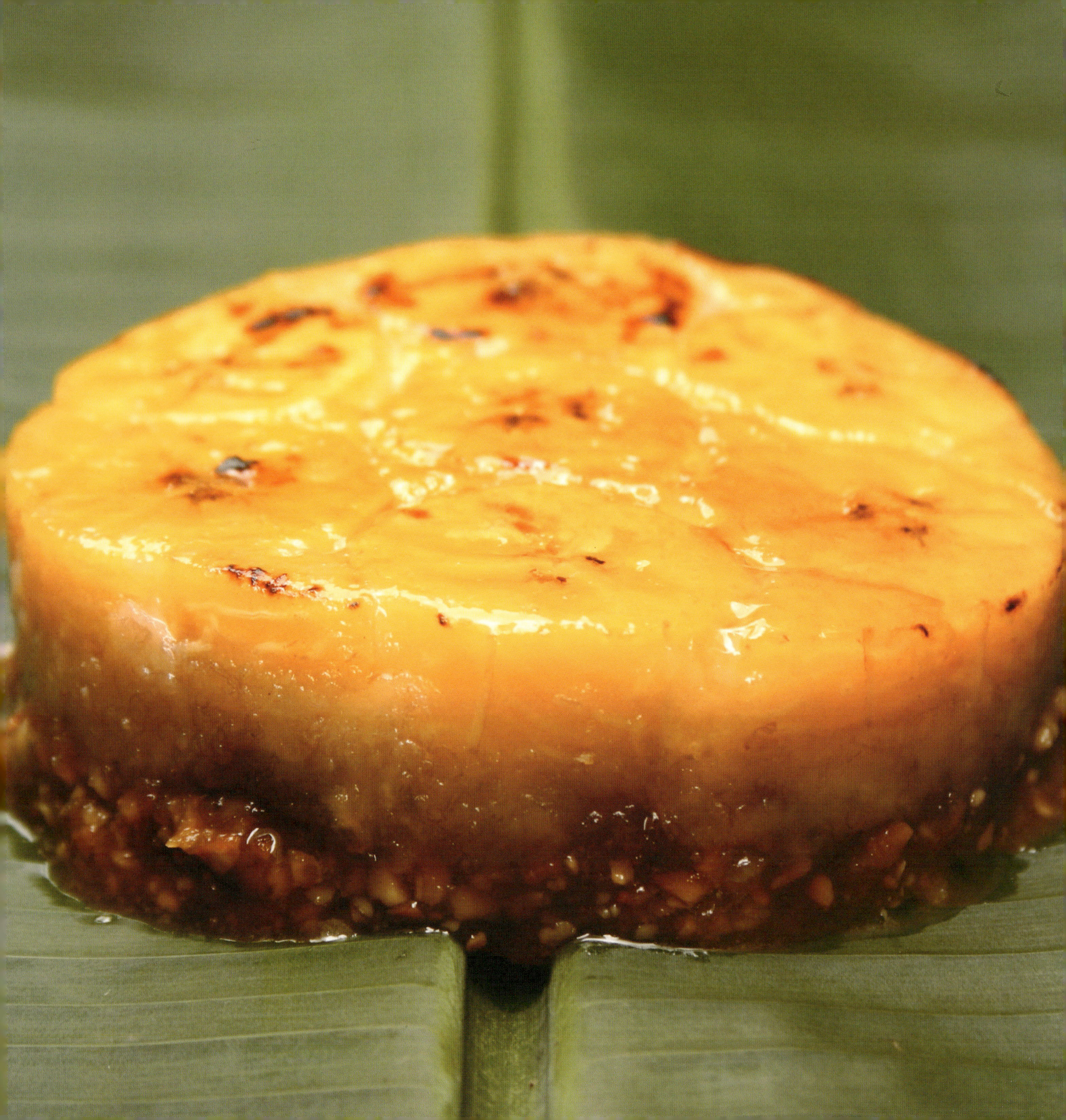

Crystallized banana pie

♪ Banana pie:
500 g bananas (3 bananas)
250 g sugar
12 bananas, to garnish
20 ml rum, to garnish

♪ Preparation: to prepare banana sweet, peel and slice bananas. Cook them with sugar for about 30 minutes, stirring occasionally until almost mashed, however, do not let it brown. Remove from heat and let cool.

♪ *Farofa*: 50 g sugar / 50 g brown sugar / 1 pinch cinnamon powder / 150 g unsalted butter, at room temperature / 150 g all-purpose flour / 150 g cashew nuts, processed into a coarse meal

♪ Preparation: mix butter with other ingredients, until you get a *farofa*, a mixture resembling a coarse meal.

♪ To assemble: cover some small round springform pans with removable base with plastic wrap. Slice bananas and place it on base of pans forming flowers. Place banana sweet and finally, top it with *farofa*. Sprinkle rum. Bake it at 180 °C for about 25 minutes. Let cool and remove from pan. Just prior serving, sprinkle sugar and cinnamon and caramelize it with a blowtorch.

♪ Suggestion: serve with cinnamon ice cream.

♪ Servings: 12 portions

♪ Preparation time: 45 minutes

Cupuaçu Pie
(Cupuaçu *is a fruit originally from the Amazon*)

♪ Crust:
300 g unsalted butter
1 egg
1 tablespoon water
700 g all-purpose flour
200 g sugar

♪ Preparation: mix butter, eggs and water. Add all-purpose flour little by little until dough achieves a firm, smooth touch, not sticky. Flatten dough with a rolling pin and cover a baking sheet. Place it in the oven for about 20 minutes. Remove from oven and leave it to cool.

♪ Cheese cream: 250 g Edam type cheese, grated / 1 can condensed milk

♪ Preparation: mix grated cheese with condensed milk.

♪ Cupuaçu cream: 1/2 kg *cupuaçu* flesh / 500 g sugar

♪ Preparation: cook *cupuaçu* flesh and sugar, stirring constantly until it acquires the consistency of a jam.

♪ Meringue: 8 egg whites / 200 g sugar / 2 tablespoons Edam type cheese, granted, to assemble

♪ Preparation: whisk egg whites and sugar for about 10 minutes until stiff.

♪ To assemble: cover cool pastry with cheese cream. Spread *cupuaçu* cream. Top with meringue, sprinkle grated cheese and place it in oven until brown

♪ Servings: 12 slices

♪ Preparation time: 2 hours

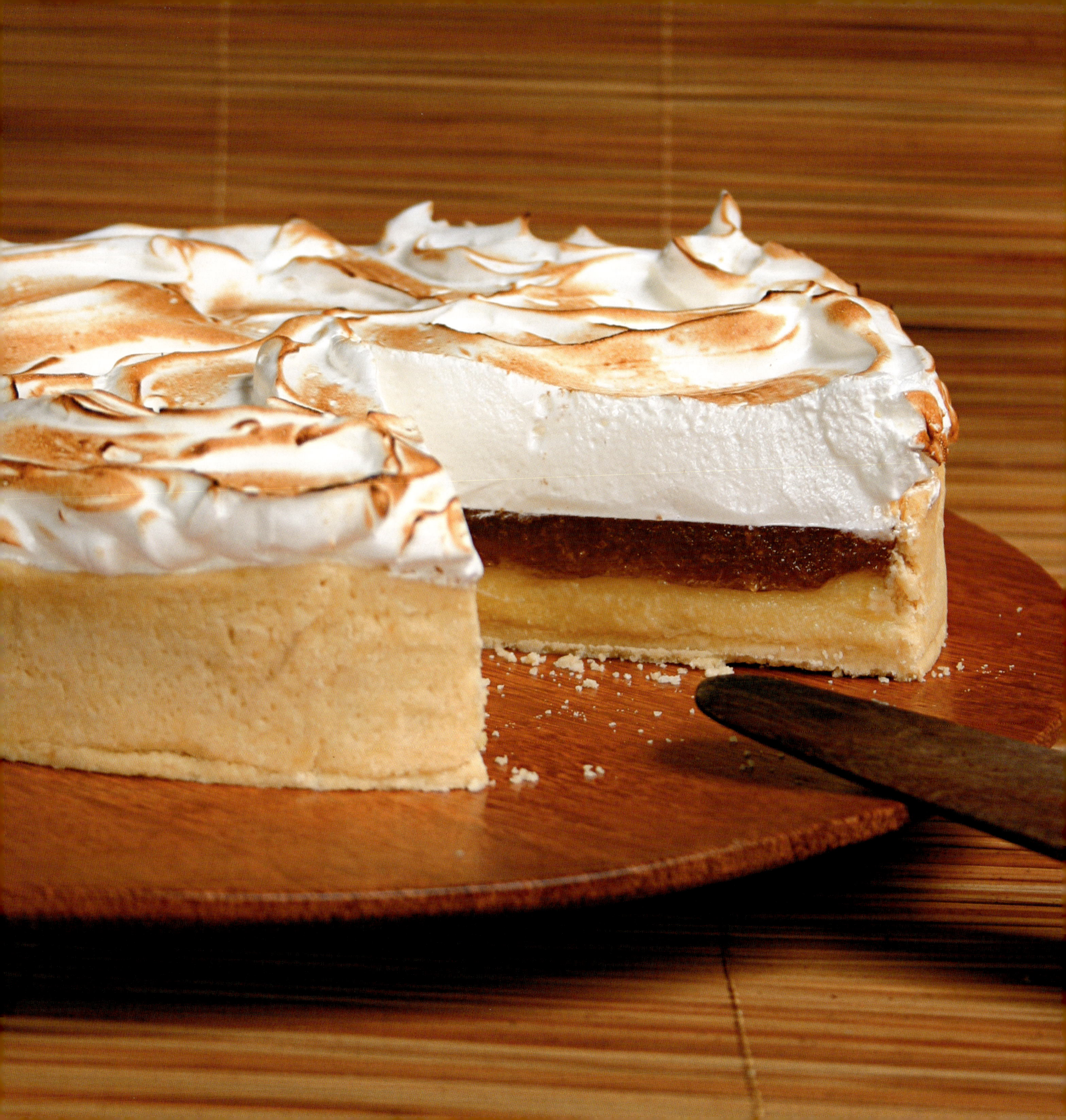

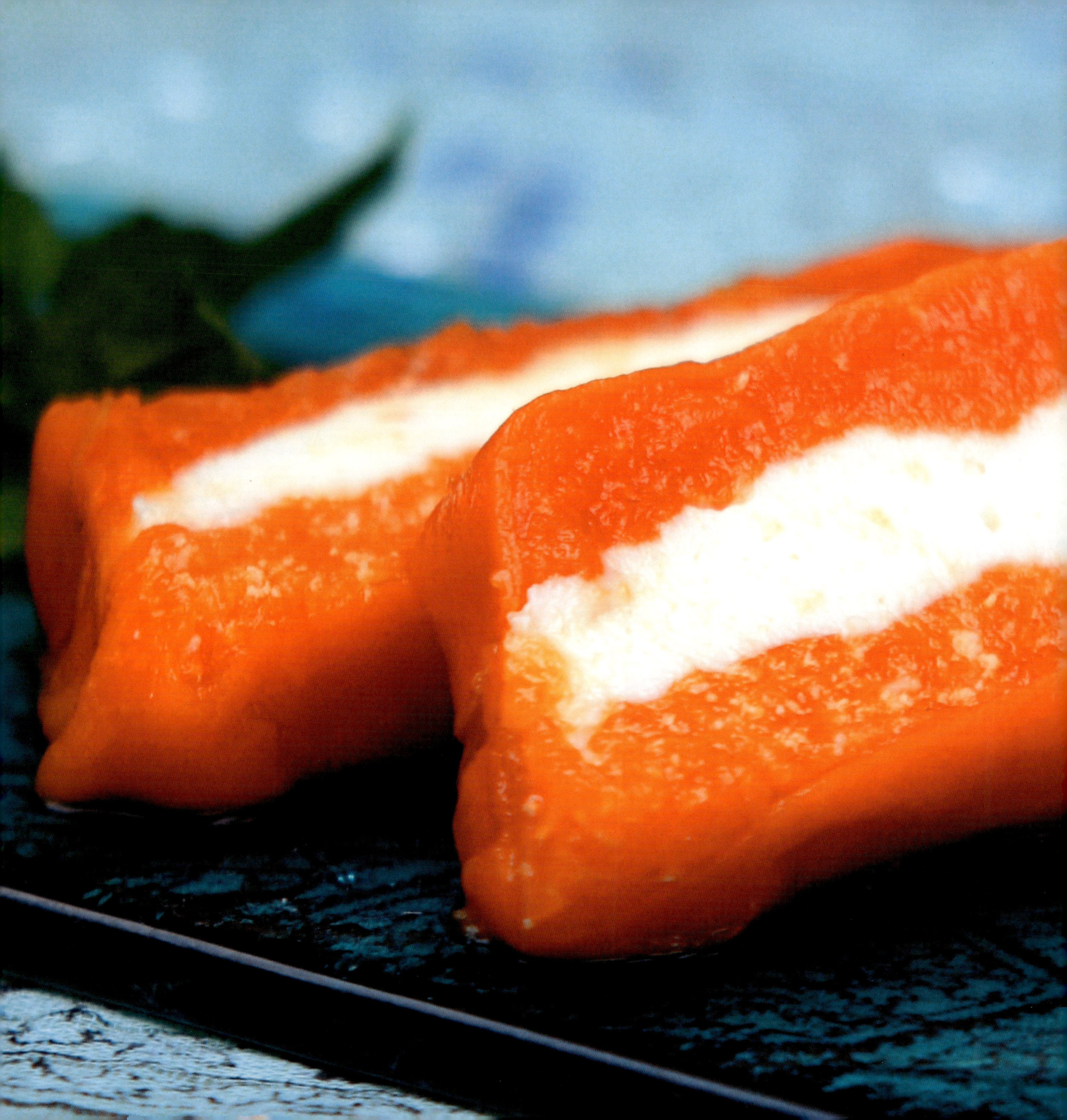

Squash and coconut terrine

♪ Squash *Carpaccio*:
800 g butternut squash, peeled
30 g sugar

♪ Preparation: slice squash lengthwise, 17 cm x 8 cm, 3 mm thick. Place in a baking sheet, sprinkle sugar and place it in the oven at 160 °C for 5 minutes.

♪ Pumpkin sweet: 900 g pumpkin / 1 *l* water / 400 g sugar / 5 cloves / 1 cinnamon bark

♪ Preparation: cook pumpkin in water, sugar, cloves and cinnamon until thick; remove from heat and set aside.

♪ Pumpkin mousse: 1 recipe pumpkin sweet (see above) / 5 sheets unflavored gelatin / 1 egg white, whisked into stiff peaks / 20 *ml* water

♪ Preparation: place pumpkin sweet in a bowl. Boil water and dissolve gelatin; pour over sweet, mixing well. Finally, add egg whites in stiff peaks, stirring delicately.

♪ Coconut mousse: 60 g condensed milk / 60 g fresh coconut, grated / 60 g coconut milk / 2 sheets unflavored gelatin / 20 *ml* water / 1 egg white, whisked into stiff peaks / 300 g cream, whipped

♪ Preparation: mix the three first ingredients in a bowl. Dissolve gelatin in boiling water, add coconut cream mixing well. Finally, incorporate egg whites and whipped heavy cream.

♪ To assemble: line a 17 cm x 8 cm metal terrine with moistened plastic wrap, leaving enough plastic overhanging on each side so as to cover terrine later. Cover base and sides with pumpkin carpaccio and spread a 2 cm layer of pumpkin mousse. Chill until firm, spread coconut mousse and chill again. Spread pumpkin mousse again. Top it with the remaining carpaccio. Wrap terrine with overhanging plastic wrap and chill. To serve, remove from pan, take plastic wrap away and slice.

♪ Servings: 12 portions

♪ Preparation time: 3 hours (not including previous preparation)

Pineapple with mint in a almond web
with ginger and coconut ice cream

♪ Caramelized almond web:

75 g almond powder
100 g unsalted butter
110 g sugar
45 g all-purpose flour
15 g ginger, grated
10 ml heavy cream
1 pinch salt

♪ Preparation: place all ingredients in a saucepan and heat. When it starts melting and thickening, remove from heat. With a coffee spoon, spread 24 spoonfuls on a greased baking sheet. With your hands, flatten them into 8 cm diameter disks, keeping distance among them. Place it into oven at 160°C for about 5 minutes. Leave it to cool and remove from roasting pan with a spatula.

♪ Marinated pineapple: 3 pineapples, peeled and diced / 300 g sugar / 10 g mint leaves, thinly sliced

♪ Preparation: simmer pineapple and sugar. Add mint leaves and chill.

♪ To assemble: form a web with caramel disks and top it with marinated pineapple. Garnish with a web triangle (1/4). Serve with coconut ice cream.

♪ Servings: 12 portions

♪ Preparation time: 45 minutes

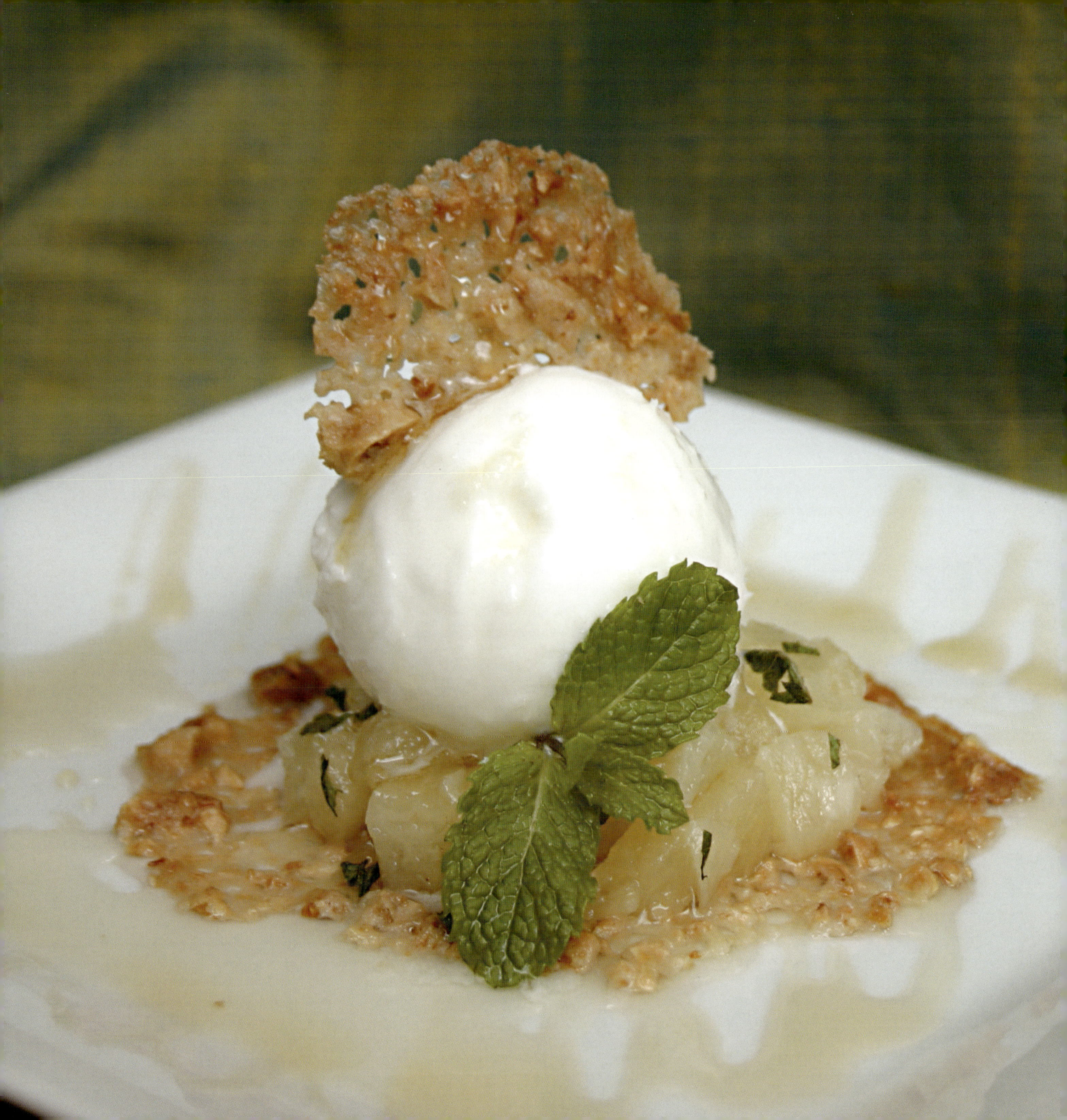

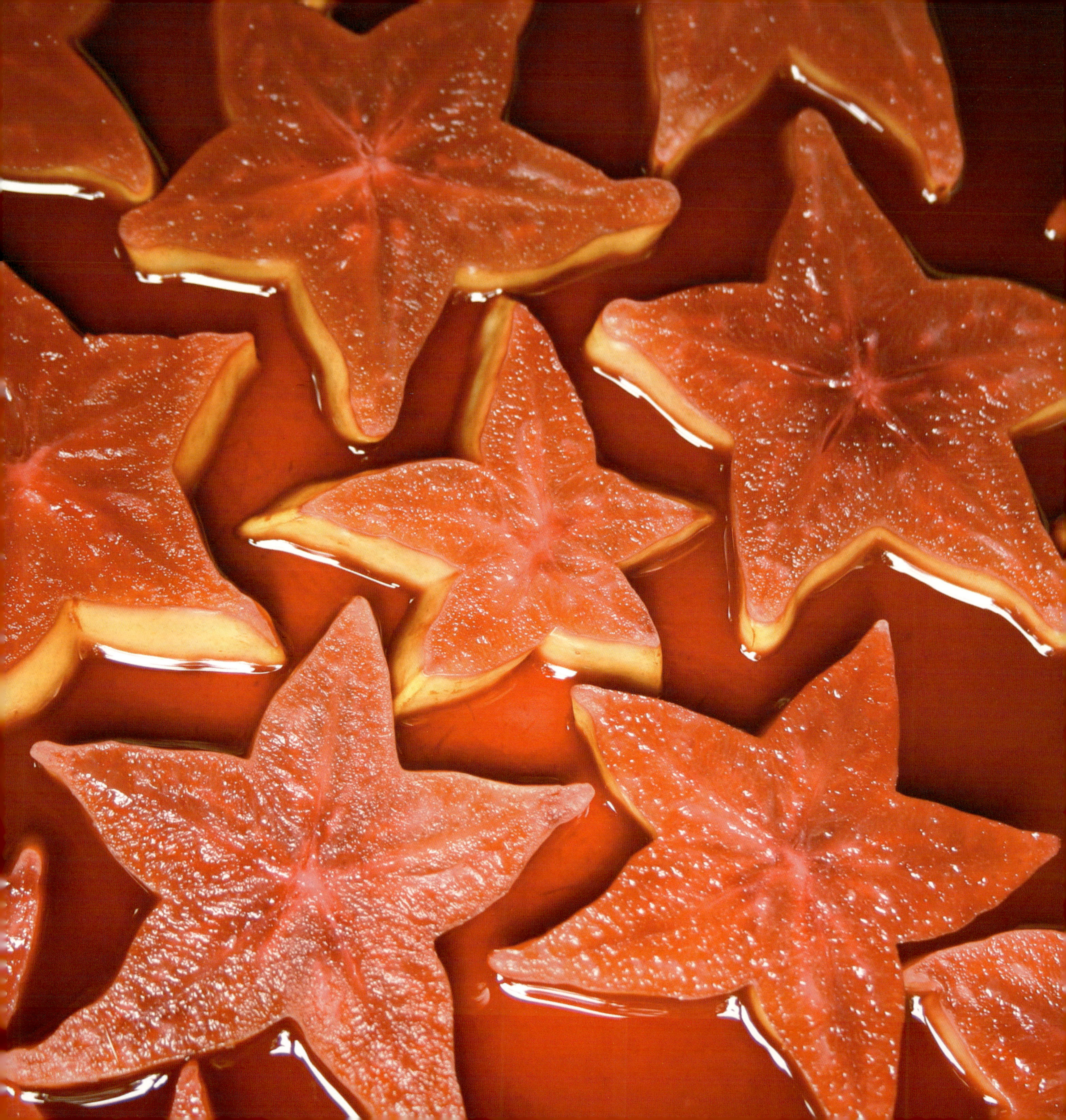

Starfruit flambéed with Port wine

5 starfruits
200 ml Port wine

♪ Preparation: slice starfruit and flambé with Port wine.

♪ Servings: 10 portions

♪ Preparation time: 15 minutes

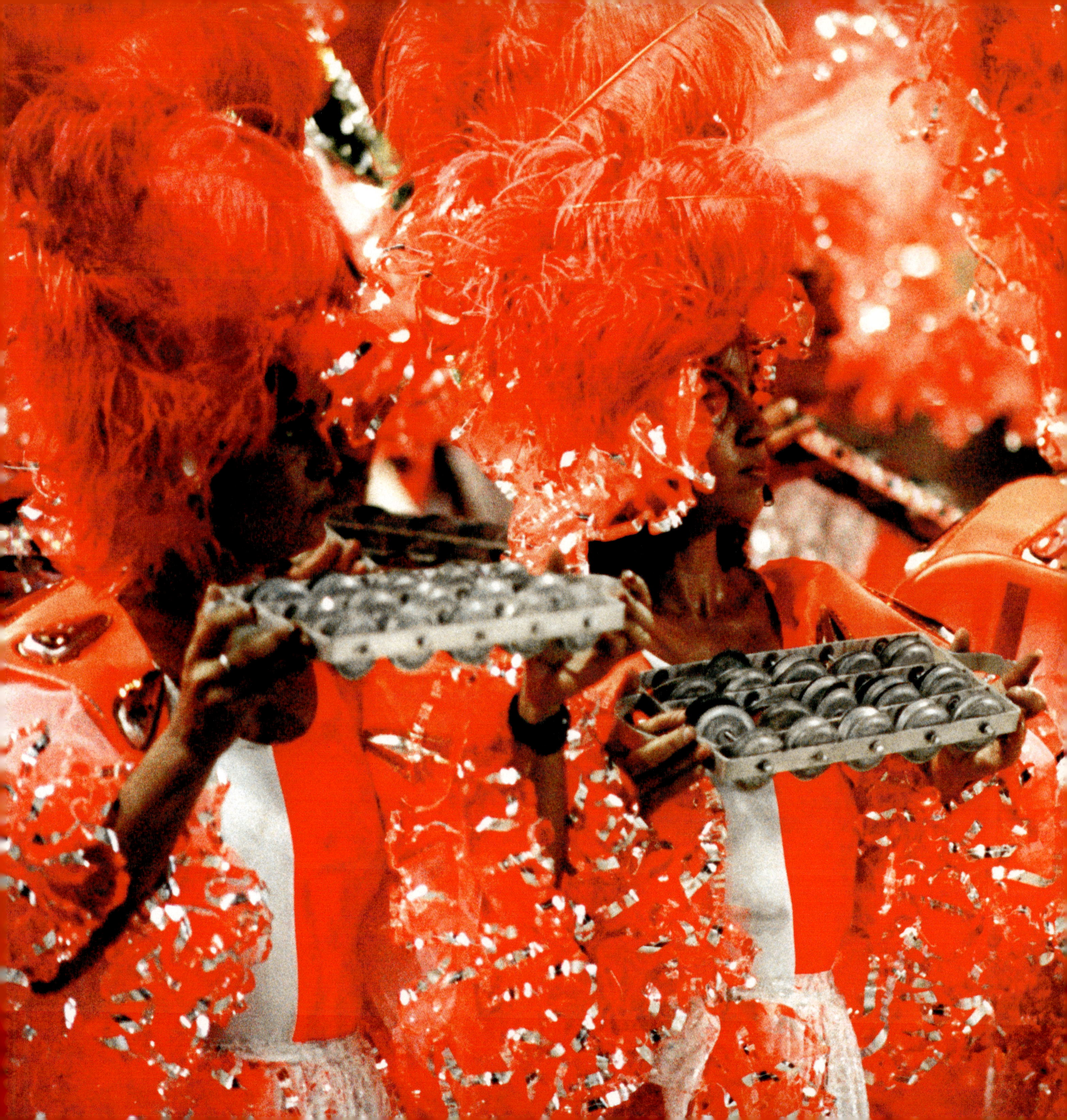

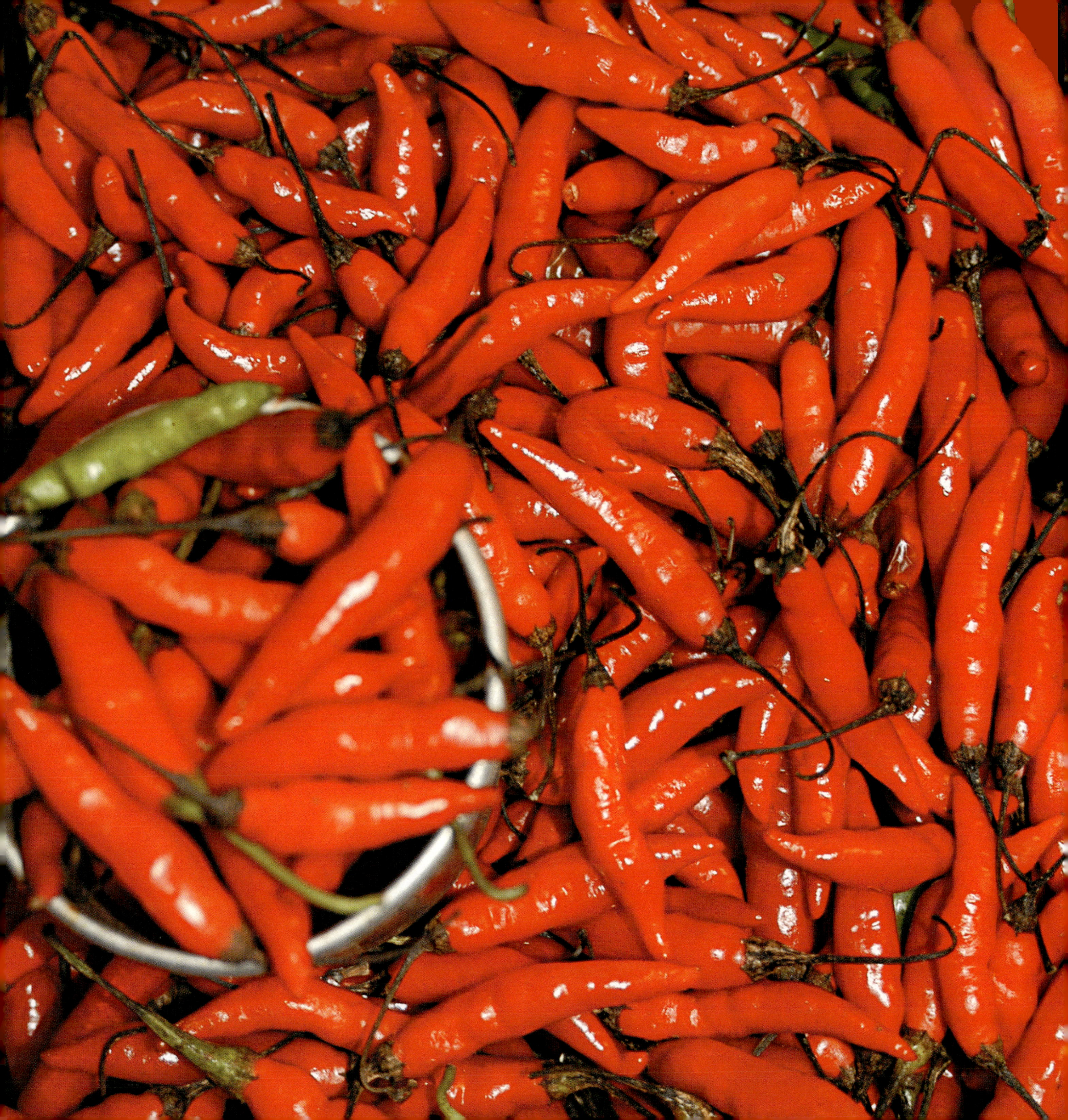

The flavors of Brazilian pop music

Specialists seem to agree that the *modinha*[1] – originated from the Portuguese *moda* and the African *lundu*[2] – is the main influence of Brazilian pop music. Surely the Indians had an ancestral custom of ritual dancing and they also used to drink and sing, making noisy drinking festivities; yet they hardly gave any contribution to the formation of our *samba*. In fact, it was the mix of melodious lyrics brought by the Portuguese and the sensual exciting rhythm practiced by the African slaves that gave shape to the typical Brazilian musicality, in a secular process involving all social segments of a forming nation.

It is said that slaves always sang while working, but it was probably some sort of ballad, almost a lament, sad and monotonous, marked by the movements of a hard labor. It is also said that women slaves would ramble the streets ballyhooing, advertising their fabric, fruits and other produce; yet, they were probably very simple, repetitive chants, perhaps a distant relative from our modern advertisement *jingles*. On the other hand, we also find in the *lundu* – satirical and irreverent – the musical ingredients that season the *modinha*, a melodious love song. On the streets and at the African *terreiros*[3], during spontaneous festivities, both white and black people danced to the fast rhythm of the *lundu baiano* reaching a climax which they called *umbigada*.[4]

The popular music that arose during colonial times, along with idiosyncrasies of a culture that blended rural traditions and urban growth, had but one delimited place with enough complexities for it to develop: the state of Bahia. This region gave birth to the musical movement that would later set foot for a wider repercussion in Rio de Janeiro, spreading Brazilian sounds and rhythms throughout the national territory, giving rise to an never-ending source of artistic creativity. It is a phenomenon that has cut across centuries and the influence of *Bahiana*[5] music can be noticed to day. The first songs composed in Bahia, usually for popular celebrations, caught the attention of elites who also took part in them, from the very beginning, without changing their basic initial traits.

This situation was favored by the peculiar socioeconomic conditions of the coast of Bahia (...) which would allow the development of various forms of entertainment among the low class, as early as in the first half of 18th century. Not only would it finally turn Salvador into the first Brazilian popular culture center, but it would also grant Bahia the title of the country's pioneer exporter of mass urban entertainment abroad.

Tinhorão, José Ramos – História Social da Música Popular Brasileira
(Social History of Brazilian Popular Music) – Ed. 34 – São Paulo – 1998, pp.82)

The thirty songs contained in the manuscript called *Modinhas do Brazil* (Modinhas from Brazil - registered by the end of 18th century and now kept by the Lisbon Ajuda Library) do not talk about food. They all refer to love, passion, longing, ingratitude: that is, emotional topics. In spite of that, considering that the aspects of everyday life would often be included in the songs, the tropical flavors must have been remembered by the early composers. Even in colonial times, there used to be many singers who usually sang solo with a guitar.

The troubadours' singing was greatly appreciated during colonial times. They performed in the streets, in homes, at festivities, and sometimes became so popular that they would go on tours around the country. Moreover, it is important to highlight that – in the *desafio*[7], also inherited from Portugal – the songs would be taken to the midlands without any titles or scores, resorting to nothing but the prodigious memory of improvisators, as master Câmara Cascudo observed: "...*viajando a pé, viola no saco de algodãozinho, aproveitando as festas religiosas, cantando nos casamentos e apartações de gado...*[8]". One of the singers from the midlands, Matias Carneiro, born in 1833, would sing:

Da macambira a farinha,
Do croatá o beiju,
Da massa de coco o pão,
Da mucunã o angu,
A melhor de todas quatro:
Croatá comido cru.[9]

Mota, Leonardo - Cantadores - Ed. Cátedra - Brasília - 1976, pp. 111

The romantic period of Brazilian imperial times[10] congregated sentimental ballads, exulting individual infatuations and putting aside the everyday urban habits. Poets began to write lyrics for melodies that were often composed by popular musicians. Shortly before the Republic, during the tumults of the Slavery Abolition days, a social countenance started to be highlighted in the songs, so much so that many scholars point this period as a significant touchstone in the history of Brazilian pop music. Often related to collective expression, though always faithful to its spontaneous irreverence, music would definitely reach the urban masses. Interestingly enough, the first hit to reach a wider public talked about the pleasure of eating outdoors. This song was intitled "A Missa Campal" (Open air mass), by Oscar Pederneiras, and described a family participation to the Abolition festivities celebrated in the city of Campo de São Cristóvão, Rio de Janeiro. In fact, it was a simple adaptation of a French chanson made to celebrate the 14th of July. The ballad, firstly performed at the vaudeville "1888" on December 27th in the Variety Show Theater, became so popular that it was later recorded by a pop singer from Bahia - 1912.

In the late 19th century, Tiradentes Square, in Rio de Janeiro, was already famous for congregating different amusement clubs, where variety shows were performed. These shows attracted people from all over the country and were excellent means to divulge new songs. Soon enough, popular composers realized that success came through the stages of the vaudevilles. Musicals covered urban types characteristically: the Portuguese and the black woman, the police officer and the scoundrel, the colonel and the hillbilly... These characters danced and sang the styles that would become popular nationwide: the *lundu*, the *maxixe*[11] and the *samba*. In the early 20th century, in a lot less provincial Rio de Janeiro, various café-concertos would manifold – for a middle class public – as well as the *chopes-berrantes*[12] – attended by poorer people. In these new entertainment houses, the most common songs were the latest *modinhas*, ballads and *choros*[13]. The modern long play had also shown up, having been introduced by the Casa Edison Recording Company (1901), which recorded *modinhas* and *lundus* performed by Eduardo das Neves. The first samba – "Pelo Telefone" (By Telephone) – would be recorded in 1917, by Ernesto Santos, popularly called Donga, a descendent of migrants from Bahia. By then the samba would acquired a drummed beat, which would turn it into the most popular kind of music in the city.

The capital of the Brazilian Republic went through deep urban changes during those first years of the 20th century. The middle class was a lot more expressive and there were many migrants from the north and northeast – mostly from Bahia – as well as European immigrants. At the café-concertos one could still listen to ballads but on the streets, the *ranchos* and *cordões* groups (the predecessors of the samba schools) had already started the *sambas* and Carnival marches. Meanwhile, in big suburban houses, women from Bahia would sing the *samba de partido alto*[14]. Rio de Janeiro was already considered as a center for music production and acquired commercial traits. Recordings and radio transmissions erupted in the 30's to supply a significant market of popular music. By the end of the First Republic[15], there was a revaluing of the national culture and its popular topics due to the centralized politics and nationalism taking place in different realms. Such exaltation could not leave our eating habits behind. Thus, Brazilian flavors come into play once again in songs by Ary Barroso and Dorival Caymmi, from Bahia.

The singer Carmem Miranda, with her tropical costumes, charmed local public and also performed in the United States, where she ended up with a great career in the cinema.

Carmem Miranda's performances drew upon the *bahiana*, that is, the woman from Bahia, a typical character created by the end of 19th century by Artur de Azevedo, when he presented the vaudeville *A República* (The Republic - 1890). In this play, the actress Ana Manarezzi, dressed up as a *bahiana* vendor, sang "As Laranjas da Sabina" (Sabina's Oranges), with the famous chorus:

> Sem banana macaco se arranja
> E bem passa o monarca sem canja,
> Mas estudante de Medicina
> Nunca pode
> Passar sem laranja da Sabina![16]

The great success achieved by singer and actress Carmem Miranda seems to close a cycle of the most glorious phase of Brazilian music evolution. Every *bahiana*, as well as the rest of the country, all the poor and lovely people sang and danced their habits, joys and even their flavors. Unfortunately, after the Second World War there would not be only one path for our music: from the 50's on, an established middle class from Rio de Janeiro would create its on music and look down on more popular varieties. The drummed *samba* and the common people's inspiration started losing ground. Then the *bossa nova* appeared, acceptably more elegant, intimate and talking about feelings. This new ode to love and flower divide the lines in a way that remains until today. Curiously enough, the guitar player who created the new rhythm was also from Bahia, more specifically from Juazeiro: João Gilberto.

Composers from more educated or refined classes would hardly ever include the flavors of Brazilian cuisine in their lyrics, either to sing out recipes or to proclaim its savours. The most relevant expressions of the "musical cuisine" often came from composers who would empathize more with the popular classes. Despite the myriad of genres and songs consumed by a real mass market, in the 60's was a clear decline in terms of mentioning eating habits in popular songs. Now and then there would be some lines in a song, yet not at all comparable to the older ballads. However, it is believed that the food topic – for its peculiarity and cultural relevance – would be cast out from popular music, and in fact, it can be found in some contemporary creation, as it is the case of this Zeca Pagodinho's song:

Já mandei botar dendê (I've asked to add dende)
(Zeca Pagodinho/Arlindo Cruz/Maurição)

Bota dendê no meu caruru	Add dende to my caruru
Bota dendê no meu vatapá	Add dende to my vatapa
Eu quero ver o caldeirão ferver	I want to see the cauldron boiling
Põe pimenta pra arder	Add pepper till it burns
Já mandei botar dendê	I've asked to add dende
[...]	[...]
Sinto saudade da comida de sinhá	I miss old lady's food
Que jamais deixou de usar	'cause she would never skip the use
Dendê pra dar bom paladar	Of dende for a good flavour
É na moqueca, é no bobó, é no xinxim	In the moqueca, bobo or xinim
Bota um pouco mais pra mim	Add a little more to me
Tempero sem dendê, não dá	Seasoning without dende won't do
[...]	[...]

It almost sounds too daring to sing the pleasures of eating and awakening the appetite for our culinary specialties, mainly in times when eating habits are more selective and restrictive. But that is the work of a *samba* player, revealing traditions of his musicality, detached from any rules outside his own environment. Both spontaneous and authentic, originally popular music sings Brazilian flavors paying homage through a melody and a rhythm of pleasure.

SANDRO FERRARI
Historian

GLOSSARY

Abará = is a dumpling made of grated black-eyed beans, similar to *acarajé*. The difference is that the *abará* is not fried, but cooked in bain marie or a double boiler then wrapped in a banana leaf.

Acarajé = is a dumpling made of grated black-eyed beans then fried in dende oil, which is then sliced in the middle and stuffed with *vatapá* and dried shrimps.

Beijú = is a kind of thick pancake made of cassava flour.

Brigadeiros = are soft candy balls made with condensed milk; they are very popular in birthday parties in Brazil.

Candomblé = is an Afro-Brazilian religion popularly practiced in Bahia, but also all over the country.

Canjerê = is the place where black magic is practiced in Afro-Brazilian religions.

Capeta lime or *limão capeta* = is a pinkish lime with very strong flavor.

Carurú = is an Afro-Brazilian dish made of okra, dried shrimps and fish, seasoned with dende oil and hot pepper.

Cavaquinho = is an string instrument seeming a small acoustic guitar with four strings.

Croatá = is a plant of the *Quesmelia liboniana* kind.

Cupuaçu = is a fruit of the Theobroma bicolor tree, originally from the Amazon.

Farofa = is prepared with cassava flour sautéed on oil or butter, and is added to numerous dishes.

Feijoada = is a very traditional Brazilian stew prepared with black beans and pork.

Macambira = is a plant of the *Bromeliad laciniosa* kind.

Moqueca = is a traditional Brazilian stew, prepared with fish and/or seafood, dende oil (palm oil) and coconut milk.

Mugunzá or *mungunzá* = is a porridge made of white corn and coconut milk, seasoned with sugar and cinnamon.

Pinyon = is a kind of Brazilian nut of the *Duguetia bracterosa* kind.

Pirão = is a traditional dish prepared with fish broth and cassava flour, and it usually goes with the *moqueca*.

Queijo coalho = is a sort of Brazilian white cheese specially made to be grilled.

Quindins = are typical Brazilian tartlets made of yolks and grated coconut.

Requeijão cremoso = is a sort of creamy white cheese.

Umbú (*Spondias tuberosa*) = is a small sweet fruit very popular in the northeast of Brazil.

Vatapá = is a typical Brazilian dish made of dende oil (palm oil), coconut milk, ginger, peanuts and is usually served with shrimp or fish and white rice.

Yellow yam or *mandioquinha* = is a typical Brazilian yam that is golden yellow, slightly sweet to taste.

---

[1] A *modinha* is a kind of sentimental love song. The *modinha* of the late 19th century was sung in the streets or as outdoor serenades, usually accompanied by a flute, a guitar and a cavaquinho.

[2] Originally, a dance performed by African slaves in Brazil, also gained popularity among the white middle class and upper crust and became Brazil's first national dance. Flirtatious couple dance, usually accompanied by a guitar, but sometimes a thumb piano or drums. Lundu is related to the Spanish *fandango* and other new-world dances like the Argentine *Zamba* and *Boleco* – they all involve, to some degree, handkerchiefs, castanets, and holding ones' arms above their heads.

[3] Place where African-Brazilian religions are practiced, even nowadays.

[4] Moment in which both dancers join each other's navels.

[5] "From Bahia". Also a woman from Bahia.

[6] Capital city of the state of Bahia, which was also the colonial capital until 1763. In 1808, when the Portuguese Royal family moved to Brazil, to escape from Napoleon, Rio de Janeiro became the capital of the colony. Brasilia became capital of the country in 1960 only, as it remains to date.

[7] An improvised competition between two popular singers, in which one singer makes up a song verse that should then be replied by the other singer.

[8] "… traveling by foot, the guitar in a cotton bag, working in religious celebrations, singing at weddings and rodeos…"

[9] "Flour from the *macambira*, / Beiju from the croat, / Bread from the coconut dough / The porridge from the *mucunã* / The best of all four: *Croatá* eaten raw"

[10] In 1822, Brazil declared its independence from Portugal and became a constitutional monarchy, known as the Empire of Brazil, which lasted until a military coup established a republic - 1889.

[11] Occasionally known as the Brazilian tango, *maxixe* is a dance, with its accompanying music, which was influenced by various other forms including the tango, lundu and polka. It is danced in a rapid 2/4 time.

[12] Popular bars to drink draft beer.

[13] *Choro* is a melodic *samba* played with a cavaquinho, a flute and a guitar.

[14] A sort of improvised *samba*, originally sung by poor people.

[15] Around 1930.

[16] "Monkeys do all right without bananas / The monarch can do without chicken soup / But no medicine student / Can do without Sabina's orange!"

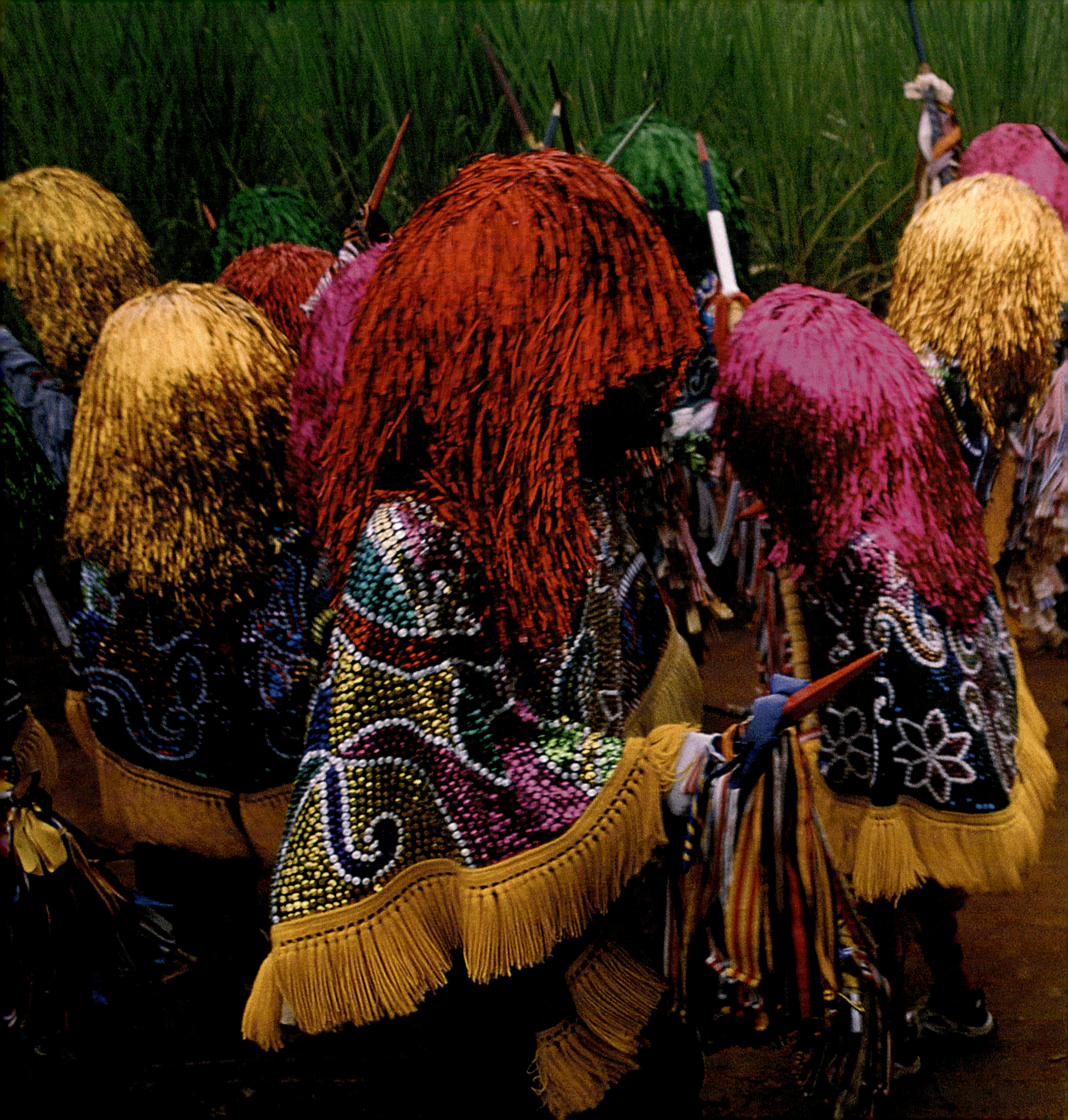

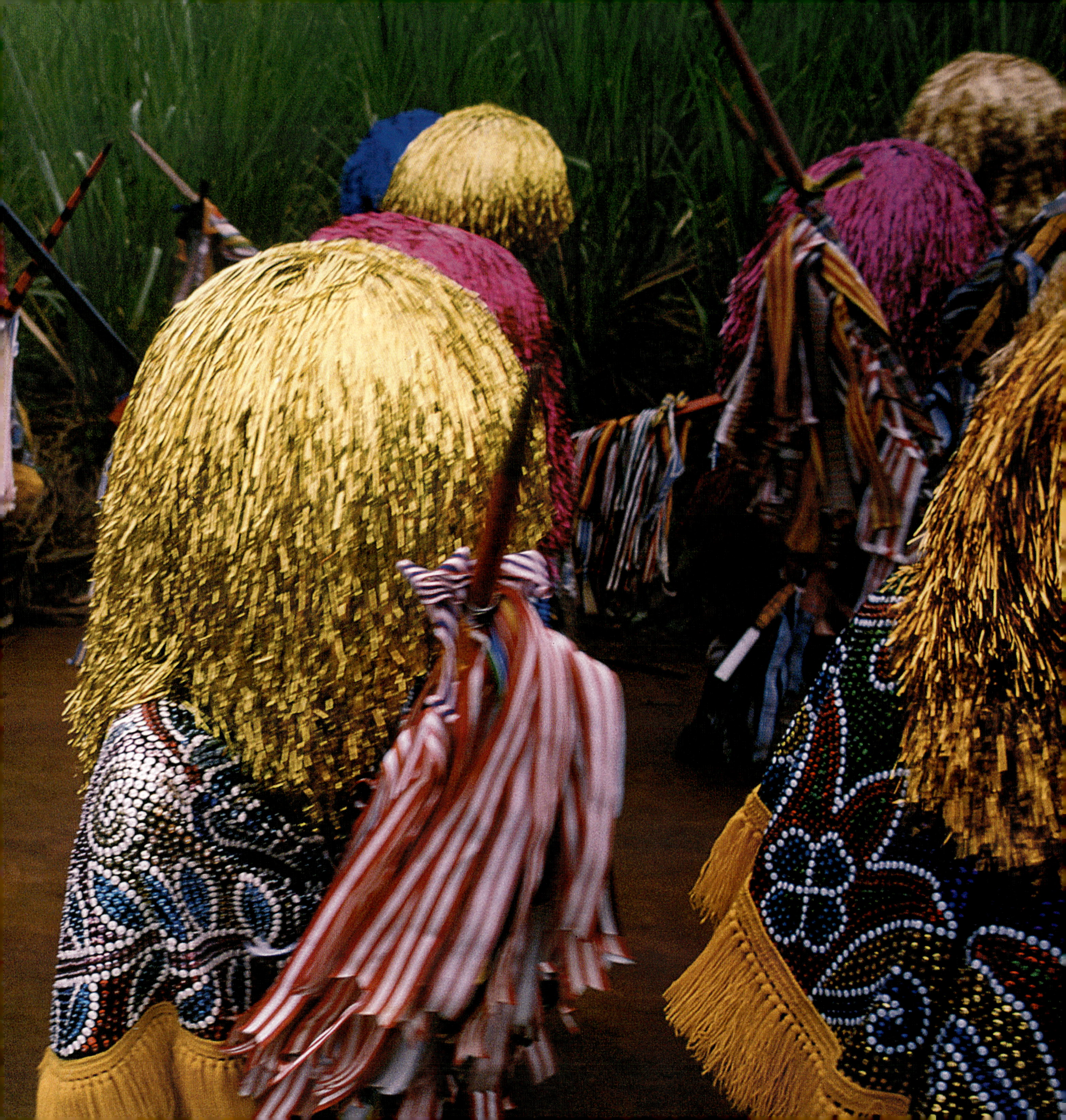

"Ai meu Deus se eu pudesse
eu abria um buraco
Metia os pés dentro criava raiz
Virava coqueiro trepava em mim mesmo
Colhia meus cocos meus frutos feliz
Ralava eles todos com cravo e azeite
E punha no tacho pra fazer cocada
Depois convidava morenas e loiras
Mulatas e negras pra dá uma provada"
♪ Antonio Vieira, Cocada

Amigos Bons : *p.* 146

Vendedor de Bananas : *p.* 148

Vatapá : *p.* 150

Feira de Mangaio : *p.* 152

Menino das Laranjas : *p.* 154

Jurubeba : *p.* 156

Banana Bacana : *p.* 158

SONGS

(141)

" Mariana Aydar comes from a new generation of Brazilian artists who are not stuck to traditionalisms. In fact, she turns any sound into music. Mariana has studied at Groove and at Berkley College of Music and has worked with young swingy people who can capture contemporary feelings and pour them into lyrics. To form her band and repertoire she creates new ways of singing famous pop songs and then composes her own with young folks. That is how, in France, she met Seu Jorge, a Brazilian singer with powerful trop cool voice, who invited her to join him on his tour to Norway, Germany and to the Bercy Stadium.

Mariana is about to cut out her first solo album and this moment has so much to do with Rhythms and Recipes. The project joins friends who came across the right path for their careers in France and who are willing to show off the wide diversity of rhythms and flavors of Brazil.

For this book, Mariana recorded a CD with producer Maurício Tagliari taking us on a trip through the Brazilian culinary universe, with new lyrics as well as old classic recorded anew. It is also a trip through the rhythms of our country, ranging from Sivuca's forró to more contemporary beats. She sets off with "Amigos bons", by Junio Barreto, which tells a story of a person who wakes up starving. Songs guide us through street vendors and fairs from the northeast, where you can buy chewing tobacco and beiju. There is also a song by Dorival Caymmi, recorded in a Brazilian beat called samba-rock, which literally teaches us how to make a vatapá. The final course is "Jurubeba", by Gilberto Gil, about a bitter liqueur made of genipap, which does wonders for hangovers. The final topping has the participation of Manga, Mariana's father, playing the guitar and the mandolin.

In her cello and guitar classes in Saint Germain-des-Prés, Mariana was sure that through her singing she could tune in to the conscience of humanity. For her, music is something spiritual, just as it had been for José de Anchieta, a clergyman and poet who was famous for um catechizing the Indians using theater and music in those first years of Brazilian history. He also lived in Trancoso and used to say that "singing makes the intelligence of heavenly things enter our souls". Five hundred years sever Mariana and Anchieta, but they seem to be finely tuned to each other. It is all about life, which can only be apprehended by those who have God in their hearts. "

CHRIS MELLO

Columnist for the O Estado de S. Paulo newspaper and Vogue magazine

(143)

Track List:

01   Amigos Bons

Júnio Barreto/Bactéria/Otto
Trama – BR-AGL-05-00015
Mariana Aydar: voice
Bruno Buarque: drums and percussion
Maurício Tagliari: guitar
Quincas Moreira: bass
Mário Manga: slide guitar
Gustavo Lenza: dubs

02   Vendedor de Bananas

Jorge Benjor
Musisom (Arlequim)
BR-AGL-05-00016
Mariana Aydar: voice
Maurício Tagliari: beats and guitar
Quincas Moreira: acoustic bass

03   Vatapá

Dorival Caymmi
Mangione, Filhos & Cia.
BR-AGL-05-00017
Mariana Aydar: voice
Bruno Buarque: percussion
Quincas Moreira: bass
Maurício Tagliari: guitars

04   Feira de Mangaio

Sivuca/Glorinha Gadelha
BMG – BR-AGL-05-00018
Mariana Aydar: voice
Bruno Buarque: percussion
Maurício Tagliari: guitar
Quincas Moreira: bass

05 Menino das Laranjas

Theo de Barros
Serasta (Fermata)
BR-AGL-05-00019
Mariana Aydar: voice
Douglas Lora: guitar
Alexandre Lora: drums
Daniel Amorim: bass
Bruno Buarque: percussion
Mário Manga: accordion and piano

06 Jurubeba

Gilberto Gil
Gegê – BR-AGL-05-00020
Mariana Aydar: voice
Maurício Tagliari: beats and guitar
Quincas Moreira: bass
Mário Manga: mandolin

07 Banana Bacana

Maurício Tagliari
Alternetmusic
BR-AGL-05-00021
Mariana Aydar: voice
Maurício Tagliari: programming, samples e percussion
Mário Manga: *cello*
Quincas Moreira: acoustic bass

Produced by Maurício Tagliari, except track "Menino das Laranjas", produced by André Magalhães • A & R: Maurício Tagliari • Technical management by Carlos "Cacá" Lima • Label manager, Chico Urbanus • Recorded by Gustavo Lenza, at YB Studios (São Paulo), except track "Menino das Laranjas" recorded at Estúdio Zabumba (São Paulo) • Mixed and mastered by Carlos "Cacá" Lima, at YB Studios

Amigos Bons

(Júnio Barreto / Bactéria / Otto) - Trama

Am
Ontem acordei de susto
Do o ronco da minha barriga com fome
Dm
Bem quando sonhava
                           Am
Que estava jantando com alguns amigos bons

Am
Salada e camurim
Cajuada aromática
Dm   **E7**   **Am**
Jenipapada e alguns amigos bons

Am
Parti
     G7   **G#7**   **Am**
Do sono da fome e da imaginação do que importa
Girei
     G7   **G#7**   **Am**
Tentando encher o que não abriga mais nada
Voltei
     G7   **G#7**   **Am**
Deitei cabeça e que olho vou e vou girar
   D7
Fica tonto depois
     Dm   **G7**   **C**   **F**   **E7**
Cai durmi volta sentir dormi dormi dormi dormi dormi

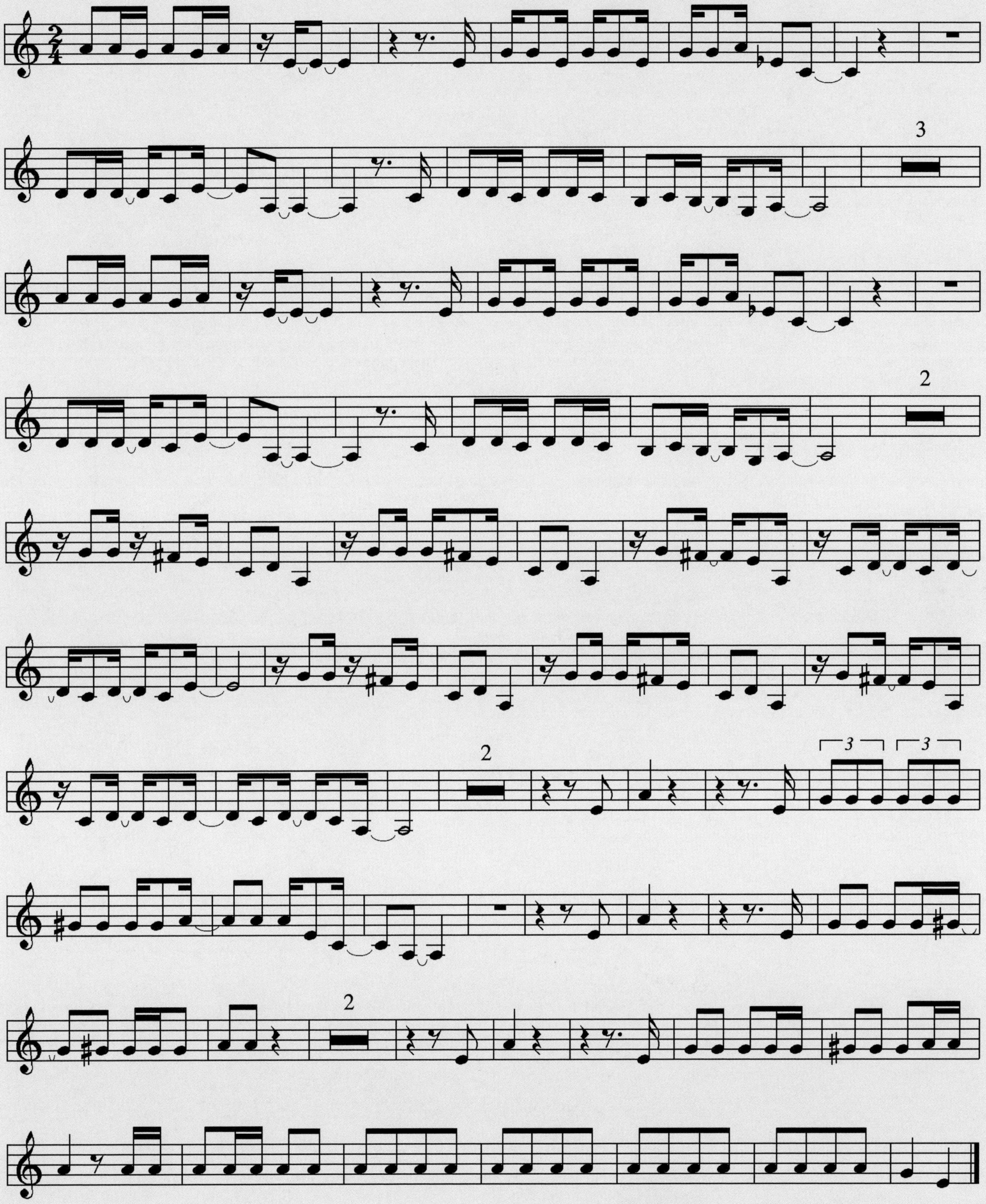

Vendedor de Banana

(Jorge Benjor) - Mussisom (Arlequim)

```
     D7
Olha a banana
Olha o bananeiro

     G7                          D7
Eu trago banana pra vender
     G7
Bananas de todas as qualidades
           D7
Quem vai querer

Olha a banana nanica
Olha a banana maçã
Olha a banana ouro
Olha a banana prata
Olha a banana da terra
Figo, são tomé
Olha a banana prata

     G7
Eu sou um menino
                       D7
Que precisa de dinheiro
                G7
Mas pra ganhar
De sol a sol
                             D7
Eu tenho que ser bananeiro
```

```
                       G7
Pois eu gosto muito
                            D7
De andar sempre na moda
                       G7
Pro meu amor puro e belo
                                    D7
Eu gosto de contar a minhas prosas

Olha a banana
Olha o bananeiro

     G7                              D7
O mundo É bom comigo até demais
     G7
Pois vendendo bananas

                              D7
Eu também faço o meu cartaz
                    G7
Pois ninguém diz pra mim
                             D7
Que eu sou um pária no mundo
                    G7
Ninguém diz pra mim
                              D7
Vai trabalhar vagabundo
Mãe, eu vendo bananas, mãe
```

(149)

Vatapá

(Dorival Caymmi) - Mangione, Filhos & Cia

```
A                Bm7
Quem quiser vatapá, oi
E7               A
Que procure fazer
F#7              Bm7
Primeiro o fubá
E7               A
Depois o dendê


F#7              Bm
Procure uma nega, baiana, ôi
E7               A
Que saiba mexer
F#7              Bm
Que saiba mexer
E7               A
Que saiba mexer


Bm
Bota a castanha de cajú
         E7      A
Um bocadinho mais
     F#7         Bm
Pimenta malagueta
         E7      A
Um bocadinho mais


D      D#0    C#m7    F#7
Amendoim, camarão, rala o coco
Bm7          E7        A       A7
Na hora de temperar
D      D#0    C#m     F#7
Sal e gengibre cebola iaia
Bm7          E7        A
Na hora de machucar


F#7              Bm
Não pára de mexer
E7               A
que é pra não embolar
F#7              Bm7
Panela no fogo
E7               A
Não deixa queimar


F#7              Bm7
Com qualquer 10 mil réis
          E7
E uma nêga, ô
          A
Se faz um vatapá
F#7              Bm
Se faz um vatapá
E7               A
Que bom vatapá
```

(151)

Feira de Mangaio

(Sivuca/ Glorinha Gadelha) - BMG

Am
Fumo de rolo
Dm
Arreio de cangalha
E7   **Am**
Eu tenho pra vender quem quer comprar
Dm
Bolo de milho broa e cocada
E7   **Am**
Eu tenho pra vender quem quer comprar

Dm
Pé-de-moleque alecrim canela
E7   **Am**
Moleque sai daqui me deixa trabalhar
Dm
E Zé saiu correndo pra feira dos pássaros
E7   **Am**
E foi pássaros voando pra todo o lugar

A7   **Dm**
Tinha uma vendinha no canto da rua
G7   **C**
Onde o mangaeiro ia se animar
F   **Bm7/5-**
Tomar uma bicada com angú assado
E7   **Am**
E olhar pra Maria do Juá

Dm
Cabresto de cavalo e rabichola
E7   **Am**
Eu tenho pra vender quem quer comprar
Dm
Farinha rapadura e graviola
E7   **Am**
Eu tenho pra vender quem quer comprar

Pavio de candieiro
Dm
Panela de barro
E7
Menino eu vou me embora
Am
Tenho que voltar

Xaxar o meu roçado
Dm
Que nem boi de carro
E7
Alpargatas de arraço
Am
Não quer me levar

A7   **Dm**
Tem um sanfoneiro no canto da rua
G7   **C**
Fazendo um floreio pra a gente dançar
F   **Bm7/5-**
Tem zefa de cursina fazendo renda
E7   **Am**
E o ronco do fole sem parar

(153)

Menino das Laranjas

(Theo Barros) - Serasta (Fermata)

    D79
Menino que vai pra feira
           Am7   **Am7**
Vender sua laranja até se acabar
    Am7   **D7**
Filho de mãe solteira
    Am7   **D7**
Cuja ignorância tem que sustentar
    D7   **G7**   **C7+** **C7**
É madrugada vai sentindo frio
    B7   **E7**   **Am7** **Am7**
Porque se o cesto não voltar vazio

       Dm7   **G7**   **C7+**
A mãe já arranja um outro pra laranja
    F7   **E7**   **Am**
e esse filho vai ter que apanhar

    Bm7 **E7**
Compra laranja menino
Bm7 **E7**   **Bm7** **E7**   **Bm7** **E7**
Bm7 **E7** **Bm7** **E7**
E vai pra feira
Bm7 **E7**   **Dm7**   **G7**   **Bm**
É madrugada vai sentindo frio
    Dm7   **G7**   **Bm**
Porque se o cesto não voltar vazio
      Dm7   **G7**   **Bm**
A mãe já arranja um outro pra laranja
    C7   **Bm**
e esse filho vai ter que apanhar

    E7
Compra laranja, laranja, laranja, doutor
Ainda dou uma de quebra pro senhor
  G7   **C7**   **F7+**
Lá no morro a gente acorda cedo
e só trabalhar
           E7   **Bb7**   **Eb7+**
Comida é pouca e muita a roupa que a cidade
manda pra lavar
           Ebm7 **Ab7**   **Db7+**
De madrugada ele menino acorda cedo
tentando encontrar
            Dm7
Um pouco pra poder viver
    G7   **C#m7**
até crescer e a vida melhorar
  Bm7   **E7**   **E7**
Compra laranja doutor
 Bm7   **E7**
Ainda dou uma de quebra pro senhor

   E7
Compra laranja, laranja, laranja, doutor
Ainda dou uma de quebra pro senhor
  G7   **C7**   **F7+**
Lá no morro a gente acorda cedo
e é só trabalhar
  Bm7   **E7**
Ainda dou uma de quebra pro senhor
 Bm7   **E7**   **E7**
Compra laranja doutor
 Bm7   **E7**
Que eu dou uma de quebra pro senhor
Seu doutor
Compra laranja doutor
Seu doutor

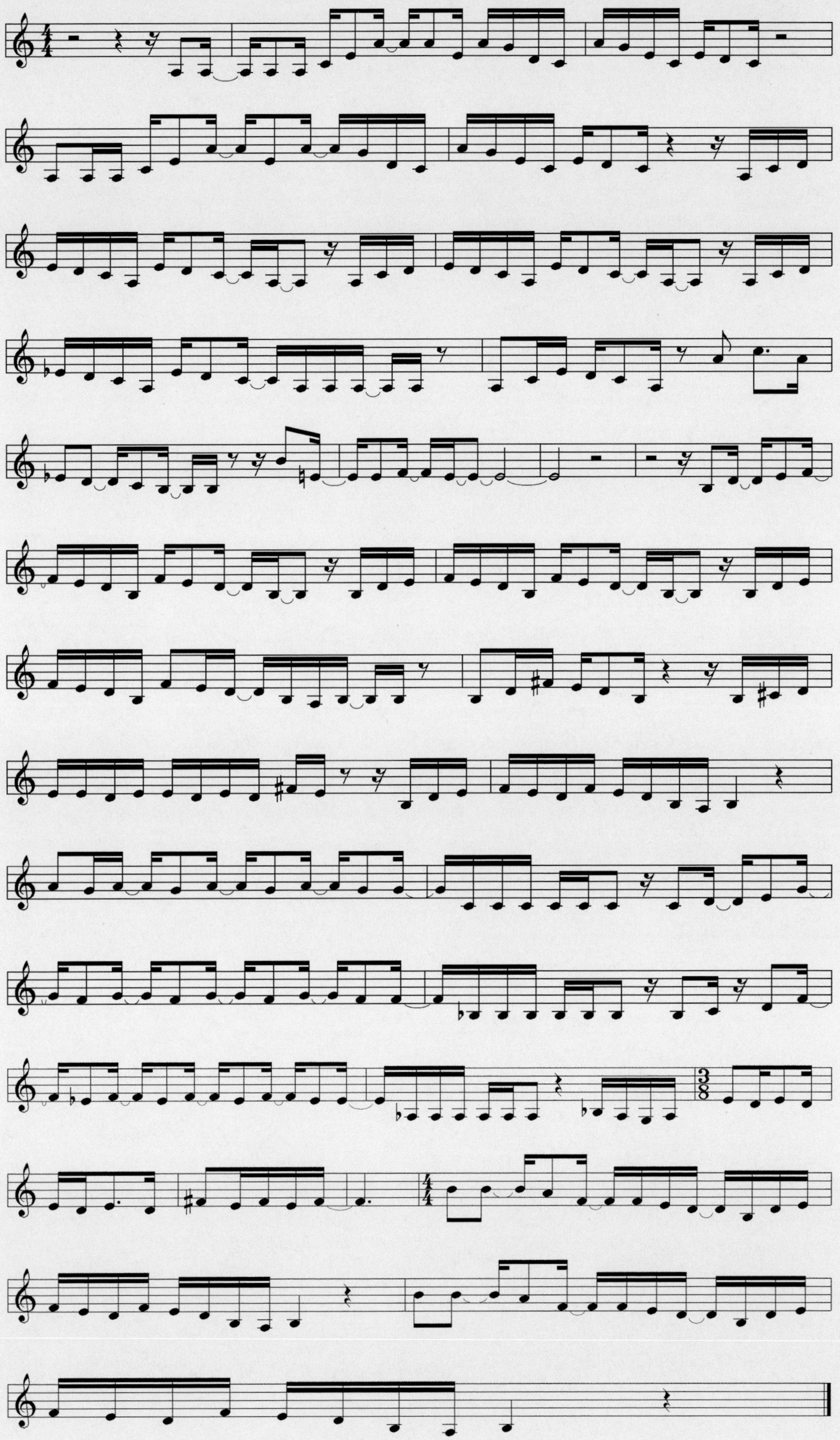

Jurubeba

(Gilberto Gil) - Gegê

B7
Juru Juru Juru Juru Juru Jurubeba
Beba Beba Beba Beba Beba Beba juru
Juru Juru Juru Juru Juru Jurubeba
Beba Beba Beba Beba Beba Beba juru

F#7   E7
Licor, Licor, Licor, Licor, Licor de jurubeba
Beba chá de juru, beba chá de jurubeba
B7
Toda bicharada viva pé de jurubeba

F#7   E7
Canta passarada linda flor de jurubeba
Quem procura   acha a cura flor de jurubeba
B7
Quem procura   acha linda a flor de jurubeba

Tudo que é de bom pro figueredo e que se beba
Feito vinho feito chá
Em licor ou em fusão
Jurubeba Jurubeba planta nobre do sertão

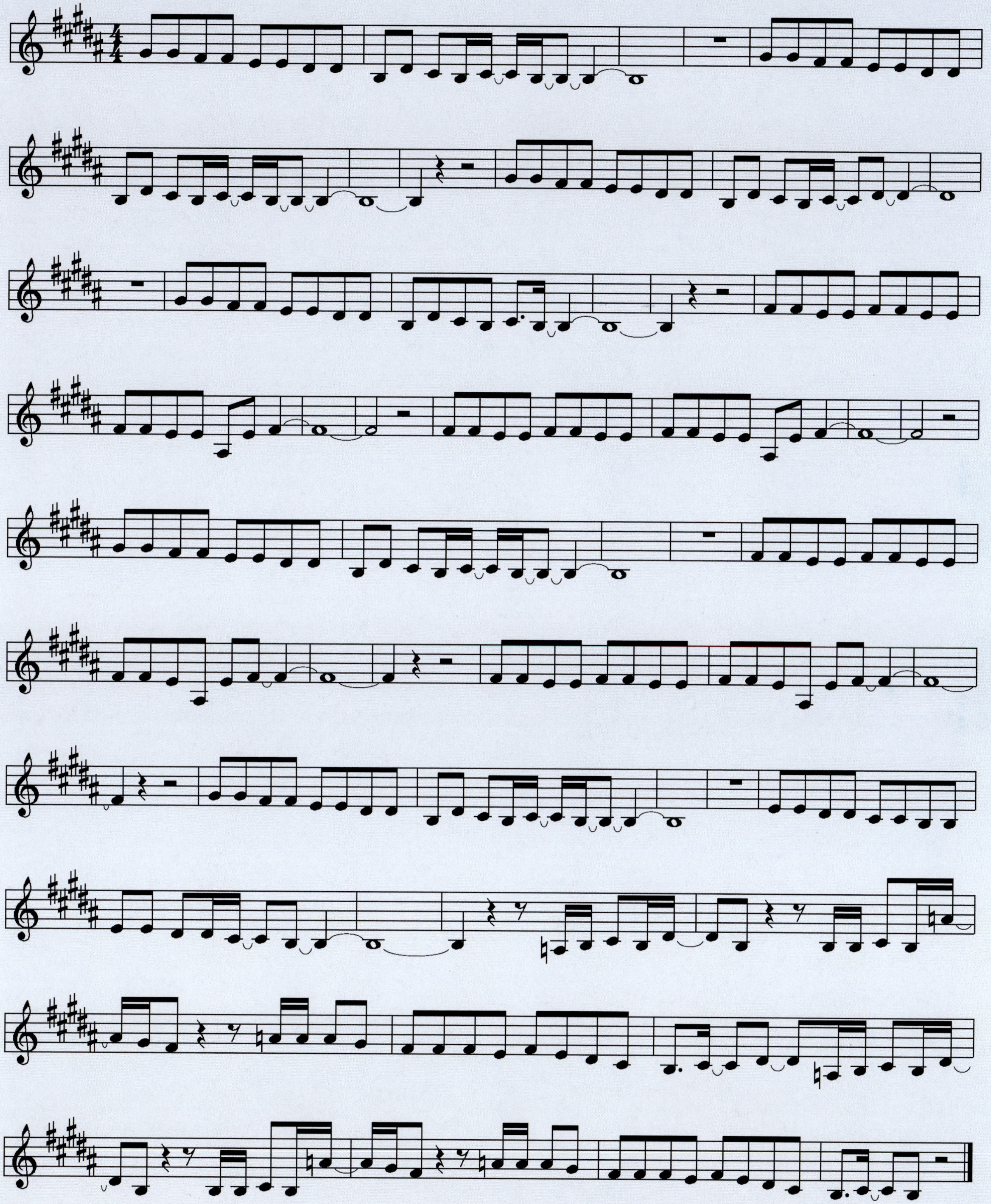

Banana Bacana

(Maurício Tagliari) - Alternetmusic

     A   A/G
De baixo do cacho da bananeira do tacho
    D
Um tacho de doce
      Dm
Num cambalacho acabou-se
    A
Diacho de vida
      A/G
A bananeira é africana
   D   Dm
O doce da cana se misturou na banana

   D   Dm
Cana banana água
   A
Inhame me ame Miami inhame me ame

  A
A cana é cubana
      A/G
Guaira guantanamera
   D
O fogo é de lenha
             Dm
E a puta é bem brasileira

  A
Do mangue do morro
     A/G
Da praia periferia
   D   Am
Da quitinete Pompéia Copacabana

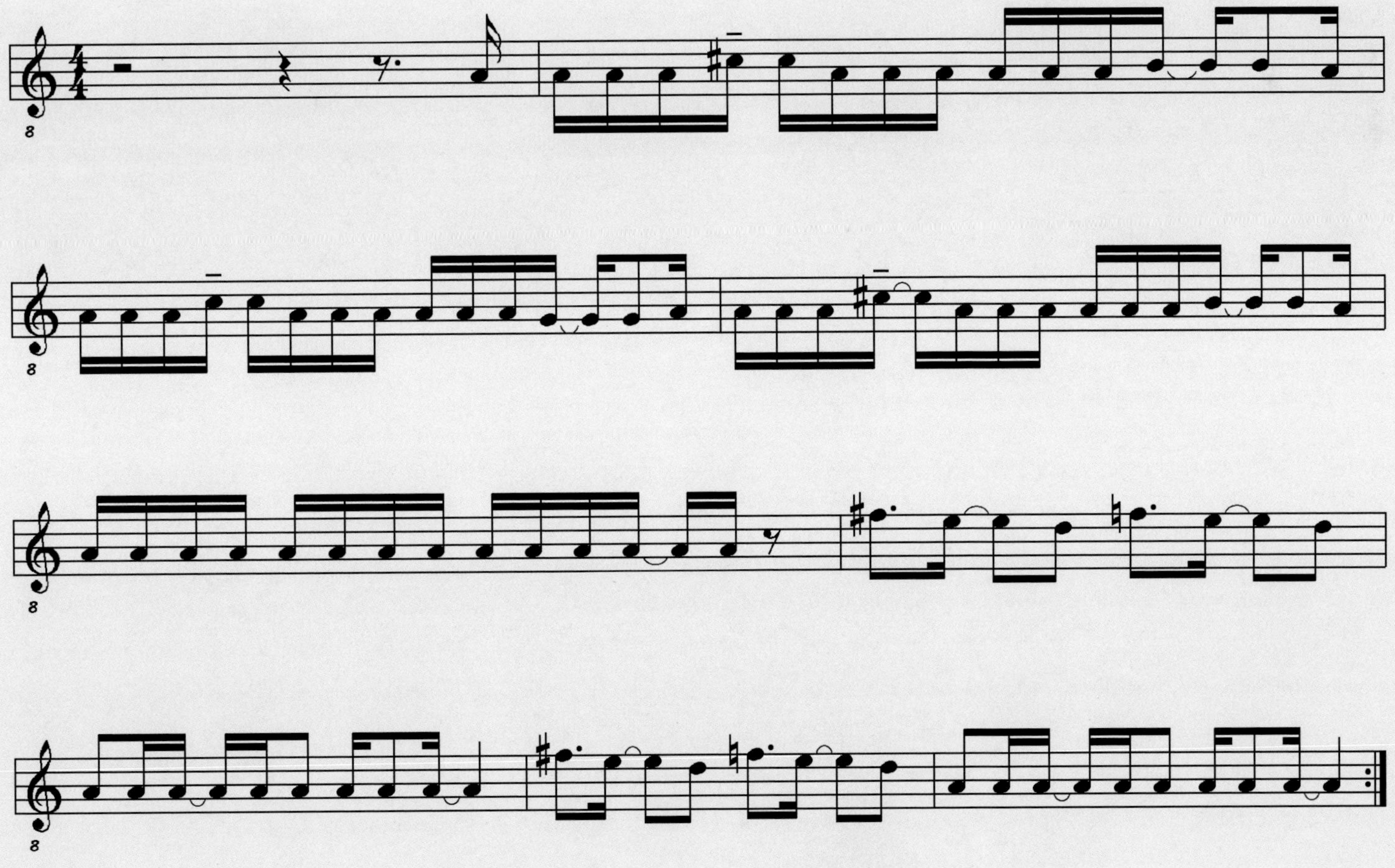
8
8
8
8

Acknowledgments

To God, for having sent me on such a wonderful journey with such a happy family, both blood family and soul family! To my parents, my brother Marcel, and my dearest grandparents • To friends, who have come to enrich my life in different moments. Estrela, Manhã, Sol, Marina, Gabu, Mel, Fábio, Naline, Aira, Renata, Celene, Fatima, Dora, Luck, Silvinha, Ana, Handolph, Ângela, Caloca, Sônia, Hugo, Rose, Baby, Isa, Nico, Martinha, Débora and family, Ana, Celina, Simoninha, Patrick, Bil, Evandro, Mariana and Sara (whom I grew up with or met in Trancoso) • Key and Charles, beautiful and dear, Roberta, Paula and Margarida (with whom I learned my second language back in England) • Sophie, soul mate, Brandine, Emiliene, Paulo, Tandi, Aglay, Rosè, Marilú, chefs Guiu, Bucheret, Terriam (with whom I mastered in my profession, in France) • Adrianas, my dear partners, friends and colleagues, my little treasures. Dado, Tininha, Alice, Tonico, Marcela, Roberto, Silvia, Estela, Flávio, Kim, Chorão, Juju, Fábio, Zé Renato, Isa, Flávia, André, Gil, Pituca, Wilma, Serginho, Alê, Edu, Méris, Eliane, Eduardo (who I met developing my passion, in São Paulo) • I could never forget Nêgo, Gisele, Cleusa, Maria, Lili, Dalva, Mili, Raquel, Fabiana, Gê, Yon, Maurício, Márcia, Cássia, Tuca, Bruno, Adriana, Edileuza,

Capim Santo, São Paulo, the restaurant where the recipes where elaborated

Jurandir, Luiz, Mel, Claudias, Cris, Geni, Erlon, Ivonete, Vera, Antônio, Alvinha, Neide, Jandis, Joaquim, Flávia, Neide, Ricardo, Rose, Júnior, Chico, Elízio, Maurício, mr. Paulino, Edu, João, Silvinho, Karen (from Capim Santo, name which as been added to mine and has become my surname), and specially Daniela, my faithful protector, ally and friend from the heart. • Finally André Boccato, my friend and editor; Camila Solla and Flávio from Casa do Design, which cared for the visual concept of the book; Karen and Airton, who made the dishes, making my ideas come true, as if they could read my mind; Emiliano Boccato, for the beautiful pictures; Rita Pereira de Souza, for all the love and support; Adriana, for the help; Myriam Khalil, for the care and dedication in the revision and translation of the recipes; Cris and Alexandra, for the historical taste; Kiko Egydio, Maurício of the YB, who fell in love with the project and produced the CD; Mariana Aydar, colleague and beautiful special friend who seasoned my recipes with songs (which adopted my dream and helped making it come true). **The book *Brazil, Rhythms and Recipes* is, thus, the result of a hard work to make a dream come true and I share it with you all who have stood by it.**

Para agendar aulas de culinária, workshops, palestras e lançamentos deste livro com a autora Morena Leite escreva para editora@boccato.com.br ou ligue (11) 3846-5141, diretamente com André Boccato.